Secret Shame

Finding Freedom by Telling the Truth

A Collection of Secrets by **Carrie Starr**

"Shame derives its power from being unspeakable." *Brene Brown*

Dedication

To Mom and Charlie, who always made me feel safe and valued.

1: The Final Exit

"Quit thinking that the battle for your heart will be a fair fight." Bob Goff

"Slam the door in his face," is my first instinctive thought.

A tall, thin man with ashy brown hair stands in front of me. He wears a white t-shirt, army jacket and jeans. He smiles broadly, asking to come in. While his green eyes sparkle with warmth, I don't trust him.

I know this man, but not really. He's familiar, like the guy who comes and reads the water meter every month. I recognize his long, thin face and the sound of his voice.

I wish I knew more about him than his physical features.

And I wish I didn't hate him.

Fifteen years of disappointment. No birthday cards. No phone calls. No ongoing communication of any kind.

But tonight he wants to be Dad again, and I'm supposed to be fine with it.

Against my better judgement, I let him in. Maybe this time will be different.

He marches confidently to our tiny, mustard yellow kitchen, slides a six pack of Budweiser onto an empty shelf in the fridge, heads to the living room and plops down on the couch. He sets his dirty work boots on the wooden coffee table, like he lives here.

Mom sits in a gold chair across the pale green living room and attempts to break the awkward silence. "How've you been, Buddy?"

Apparently, people call my dad Buddy instead of Charles or Charlie. It was a nickname he acquired during his childhood, something I know almost nothing about. He's everyone's buddy, except ours.

"No complaints. How are things here?" Dad asks.

My older brother and I have absolutely nothing to say. We've gone through this polite charade before. We are tired of it. Dad occasionally acts interested in our lives after a fight with his second wife. She kicks him out of the house, again. He gets drunk, again. He inevitably lands on our doorstep, again.

When it's convenient, we exist. At least for the evening.

"Carrie just got accepted into the Spanish Honor Society," my mom offers cheerfully on my behalf.

We can always count on Mom to celebrate our accomplishments. Dad doesn't know about them. There is rarely an opportunity to inform him of family news since we have no means of contacting him. Maybe he'll actually care. Maybe he'll be proud and say, "Congratulations! That's so wonderful!!"

I allow a tiny glimmer of hope to rise up within me.

"Of course she did. She's *my* daughter isn't she? She's got good genes. I expect nothing less. I always did well in school. Smartest kid in my class. Why do you think the Marines chose me for Intelligence? When I was serving overseas....."

...and Dad launches into a long, animated story of his all-time favorite subject: himself. An hour goes by and our eyes glaze over. We try our best to listen politely.

We have been raised to be polite. Kind. Courteous. Even when the person in front of us is acting like an imbecile.

Suddenly, Dad leaps off the couch. "Charlie, punch me! Go ahead and hit me in the gut. Hard as you can, son. Go on. Hit me!"

My brother is my dad's namesake, complete with the same long face and thin build.

"No thanks, Dad. I'm going to bed," my exhausted teenage brother answers.

"Come on. Hit me." He lifts up his white t-shirt and starts punching himself in the abs. "Hard as a rock, I tell ya."

"Fine," my brother concedes, accommodating as we've both been taught to do.

Charlie hits him with an obligatory punch in the stomach. We all feign shock and awe at Dad's six pack of steel. We know that's the only way this show ends.

Dad sticks up his pointer finger, then thrusts his arm out, fully extended. "Ya gotta look out for number one kids. Always look out for number one. No one else is gonna do that for you. I always take care of number one."

Yes, we know. All too well.

Charlie and I head off to bed, expecting him to leave.

The next morning, Dad is still there flirting with Mom at the kitchen sink.

Dad doesn't typically stay over. He shows up unexpectedly, spends a few awkward hours with us and leaves again, usually for years.

But this time, he stays. All night. All weekend. All week. I hate it. I hate it with everything in me. I don't understand why he's allowed to stay, but I don't ask. It's not my place.

"Walk on my back Carrie," he demands one afternoon.

"What?" I ask, confused. Dad lays face down on the olive green carpet in the dining room.

"Don't worry. You're a tiny little thing. You won't hurt me. Now, walk on my back. Your mother's bed is killing me."

At fifteen, I weigh 95 pounds. My family is worried I'm anorexic, but I'm just plain skinny. Being called a "little thing" by my father makes me feel uncomfortable. And I don't want to think about him staying in my mom's bed.

My mother holds my hand to balance me as I awkwardly step onto his bony frame. I can feel his ribs and spine through my socks.

The next day I come home from school and find a black, army-style foot locker in our living room, full of Dad's stuff. He has officially moved in. Is he crazy?

He starts helping with the cooking and washing the dishes. He makes repairs around the house. He sits on the couch with his arm around my mom. It's unsettling.

It feels as if I've been transported into a science fiction film. My father is ET, a strange guest who will inevitably leave us once we become attached.

My goal is to stay unattached.

I hang up "No Smoking" signs around the house. I blast music from my record player while he watches TV. When he walks into a room, I walk out. When he leaves a half empty can of beer on the coffee table, I pour the remaining contents down the drain. I don't want him living in our house.

"That daughter of yours is a little bitch," I hear him tell my mom.

"She never acts like this," my mother insists. "She's only like this around you. She's usually very sweet."

My dad tries to enforce a new system of chores. He wants my brother and me to help out more around the house. I point to the chore chart on the fridge and insist our family is functioning just fine without him. We don't need his help. Why is he acting like he's in charge? This is not his home. We don't want him here. He is welcome to leave anytime!

I stomp out of the room furious. Who does he think he is, finally trying to be a father after all of these years?

Unbeknownst to me, my dad starts crying. I've already left the room, but he confides in my mother. My words have actually hurt him. They've cut through the tough-guy facade. He doesn't like being unwanted and unwelcome.

A few nights later he puts a folk album by Peter, Paul and Mary on the record player. He and my mother start singing along after dinner. They sound beautiful together. I try to give Dad my typical cold shoulder, but something begins to soften inside me.

After several evenings of this routine, I find myself sitting at the table, singing along with them. With Dad's deep bass and Mom's alto, I add my soprano, and we start singing in three part harmony. Again I've been transported into the scene of a movie. Not science fiction this time. Maybe more of an epic drama. Or at least a TV episode of Family Ties. Perhaps Michael J Fox will stop by and add some tenor?

Dad introduces me to his favorite song, American Pie by Don McLean. He shares the political backstory of the lyrics and explains every character in detail. It's sad and haunting and intriguing. We sing it over and over again until I have every word memorized. It's a marathon song, and we sing it to the finish line together. He looks at me and smiles with pride. The feeling is so foreign, I almost don't recognize it. For the first time, I bask in my father's approval.

One afternoon Dad runs out to his car and grabs a book off his dashboard. He brings it to me in the living room, short of breath. He places it in my hands, claiming it's the best book he's ever read. Knowing my love of reading, he tells me I can keep it. I stare at the cover and marvel. It's the first gift I ever remember him giving me. I carry it to my room and place it on my nightstand, a rare treasure.

At school I mention to a friend that my parents will be coming to our chorus concert that night. The word *parents* catches in my throat. "Parents?" she asks. I realize how strange it sounds. She only knows my mother. Mom comes to everything I do, alone. No one has ever met my dad. I suddenly feel normal to have parents, plural.

Weeks later I stand in the yard in my pink prom dress. It's long and full with matching pink lace around the edges. My hair is professionally styled in curls all pinned up on my head with tiny baby's breath flowers tucked all around. Dad insists on having his picture taken with me, "looking so beautiful." He puts his arm across my shoulders, and I smile. My father, absent for so long, is finally here. He knows me. We both like to sing and read, and he thinks I'm beautiful. I never knew.

Mom and I are active in our church, and we recently lost our pastor. He was called to a new congregation out of town, and we miss him and his family. We decide to plan a weekend trip to visit them, and I can't wait!

Mom and I enjoy the time alone in the car, singing along with the radio. We stay at our friend's house. It's a beautiful, sunny spring weekend. We go to the mall together and buy ice cream for dessert after our lunch. The next day, Mom and I attend their new church, and we're truly happy for them to be serving such a friendly congregation.

We return home excited to tell Dad and Charlie all about our weekend adventure. When we enter the house, only my brother is there. I look in the refrigerator. There's no beer. I check the living room. Dad's foot locker is gone.

There is no note. No phone number. We don't even know where he lives.

I wait for days for him to come back. To call us. Anything.

I wait for weeks.

I wait for years.

Nothing.

This time, he has left for good.

All I have left of my dad is the book on my nightstand.

It's the worst gift he ever could have given me.

2: Man in the Mirror

"Trust is built in very small moments." John Gottman

"There's a stranger in our house," I nervously whisper to no one at all.

I sneak down the hall on my little tiptoes, afraid of what I might see. A deep voice is coming from Mommy's bedroom. Is it a robber? A murderer? Mr. Ferris the plumber? It's unusual to hear a man's voice echoing down our narrow hallway.

Mommy's bedroom door is open. I creep closer, and the thick scent of cheap cologne assaults my four-year-old nose. I peek around the corner through the doorway. A tall, thin man with mousy brown hair and a white dress shirt is standing in front of the mirror, straightening his long black tie.

I pause, staring for minutes, confused by what I see. Who is this person all dressed up and fancy in Mommy's bedroom? Why is he here? Why does Mommy appear so comfortable and at ease with this stranger standing so close to her? Should I scream and wake up Charlie?

When Mommy finally notices me, she introduces the man in the mirror as "Daddy." He slept over with Mommy the night before and is now getting ready for work at the bank. Her words are very matter-of-fact, as if this is perfectly normal.

This is not the way a daughter should meet her dad.

The relationship between a father and his daughter is precious. Or at least it should be. Today I have two daughters of my own who are fabulously loved by their father. A daughter is a princess in the eyes of her father—a precious treasure to protect.

I never felt protected or provided for by my dad. In fact, I grew up feeling quite the opposite. Abandoned, ignored, and neglected.

Certainly I'm not alone in feeling this way. I've met countless others who have never known their father's love. Some never knew their father at all. Others were discarded by their dads at some point during their childhood. And still others have lived with their fathers present their entire lives and yet they never really felt his presence.

I've seen this happen with absent moms too.

Decades after that initial encounter with my dad, I still long to know that elusive man in the mirror. I'm amazed at the number of people I've met who struggle with being neglected by a parent. Whether it be a single hurtful incident or a lifetime of pain and disappointment, they are defined by it. They cannot see past the tragic experience, and it holds them captive.

Being fatherless defined me as well. It owned me. The fancy man I met at four-years-old disappeared as quickly as he'd arrived. Years and years would go by before I saw him again. Because of my father's absence, I convinced myself I was no one's precious princess. I believed I was an inconvenience- easily forgotten and easily discarded. And it became my identity.

3. Welcome Home: *Aubree's Story*

"Love is uncertain. It's incredibly risky." Brene Brown

Aubree lives in a family of four with her mother, twin brother and older sister. Her Dad is never around. He can't be because he's in prison. She doesn't know him at all. She doesn't even know what he looks like.

Until now.

Aubree is in third grade and her mother has a difficult decision to make. Her ex is about to be released from prison and has nowhere to live. He's fathered a total of twelve children, nine other than her own. The three other mothers are unwilling to take him in. She feels guilty denying Aubree and her siblings the chance to know their dad. She decides she will allow him to move into their home.

Aubree's mom picks him up from prison after work at the factory. Next she picks up Aubree and her siblings from the babysitter. The kids have no idea who the man in the front seat of their family van even is. Her mom introduces him as their dad. To Aubree, he has appeared out of thin air.

He begins living in their house five days a week. The other two days, he has to be back in prison. Eventually, he is let out on parole and lives with them full-time. The emotional abuse starts immediately. His words are cruel and harsh.

Aubree is asthmatic, and her dad is a smoker. Aubree's mother asks him not to smoke in the house because it's dangerous for their daughter. He ignores her and smokes in the house whenever he wants to anyway. The smoke starts to make Aubree sick, but her dad doesn't seem to care. His habit is more important than her health. Eight-year-old Aubree ends up spending a week in the hospital because she can't breathe in her own home.

Aubree wants to love her dad. Sometimes he can be really fun. He takes her to a NASCAR race, and they have their photo taken together. It's the only photo of the two of them together she's ever owned. It's one of the happy days. The highs with her dad are really high, but the lows with her dad are really low.

Her older sister gets smacked around a lot, and Aubree hates it. Her brother gets picked up one-handed by the neck and slammed into the fridge on Super Bowl Sunday. It's not the only time she sees him treated this way by their father.

The presence of Aubree's dad seems to bring out the worst in her mom. More than once Aubree gets off the bus after school and finds them both hanging out drunk in the driveway. She's scared but doesn't know what to say.

The summer after 5th grade, Aubree's mom and her grandfather leave town for a vacation, leaving Aubree and her siblings in the sole care of their father. They hope it will be fun having Dad in charge while Mom is not around.

Her grandfather gets very sick, and her mom needs to stay out of town for months while her grandfather recovers. While they are away, her dad brings Aubree, her brother and her sister to stay at a friend's house for weeks at a time.

They later find out her dad is having an affair with their mom's best friend.

Though he lives in the same house, Aubree's father has no idea when her birthday is. He doesn't even know how to spell her name. After two long years of neglect and abuse, her dad disappears completely.

At just ten years old, Aubree has a fractured family again. She is left feeling bitter and confused.

Her dad is still nowhere to be found. She has not seen him since the day he left. For many years, she was terrified of seeing him. All through middle school and into high school, Aubree feared her dad would come and take her away.

She became paranoid about her dad, not knowing when or where he might show up in her life again. Even in college, she was afraid her dad would come up behind her in the dark and abduct her. She still fights those fears today.

The emotional wounds her father inflicted during those two short years left her frightened and anxious. The damage done by leaving and never returning left her lonely and longing for her father's love. She spent years trying to fill that void with bad relationships and unhealthy decisions. To this day, she doesn't know where he lives, his phone number, his email. Nothing. All she knows is his name.

She is broken but has started rebuilding. Hers is a life defined by moving three steps forward and two steps back. She is learning confidence and freedom, but she is frequently preoccupied with thoughts of her missing father.

4: Sweet Love Story

"There's some people in this world who you can just love and love and love no matter what." John Green

My father eluded me most of my life. Like an actor on a screen, he seemed real but there was no way to actually get close to him. Never leaving a phone number to call or an address to visit, he seemed a figment of my young imagination.

He was an enigma to my mother as well.

My parents went to the same small-town high school but weren't really friends until Mom went off to college. Dad never enrolled in classes but instead enlisted in the military. He was strong, intelligent and charming. He was a bit of a troublemaker, but my mom found him intriguing and exciting. She believed he was as Sweet as his last name.

My mother was smart, well-organized and social. (She still is!) She loved to host events and brought laughter and joy to any room. She was playful and optimistic, and he found her delightful. He proposed her senior year of college.

While she excitedly said "yes" to his proposal, not everyone was thrilled about their engagement. He was also unstable, irresponsible and a flirt. My grandparents didn't trust him.

My parents were married shortly after Mom's college graduation. She started her first teaching job, and their wedding was held on Thanksgiving Eve, allowing them a four-day honeymoon in New York City. It was a beautiful, candlelight ceremony. If you look at the pictures, neither of my grandparents are smiling.

When my mother was a senior in college she started having headaches. Excruciating headaches. Sometimes the pain would be so intense she would wrap a belt around her head and tighten it in attempt to relieve the pressure. She visited several doctors, but none of them could discern the cause of her extreme pain.

While my parents were still newlyweds, my mom was diagnosed with AVM's, a malformation of the blood vessels in her brain. They were twisted together, forming a mass of pressure inside my mother's skull. The only treatment was high-risk brain surgery. Mom survived two invasive procedures within the first two years of their marriage.

While the groundbreaking surgeries brought an end to the headaches, they forever impacted my mom. The brain is an incredible masterpiece of complication. Once it's injured, it's almost impossible to repair. The extensive rehabilitation following her surgeries required her to learn to talk, walk and read all over again. As you can imagine, this put tremendous strain on her young marriage.

Dad struggled with faithfulness from the beginning of their union. He had a wandering eye and a discontented heart. He'd work late hours and sometimes weekends yet my mother trusted him. He had a talent for stretching the truth.

The day my mom discovered she was pregnant with me, my dad and his coworkers from the bank hosted an impromptu celebration at a local restaurant. After dinner, one of Dad's coworkers excused herself from the table. She was gone for quite some time. My father feigned concern and offered to go check on her. When neither my father nor the woman returned, my mom began to worry and went searching for them both.

What my mother discovered would change the course of her life forever. She found my father and his co-worker passionately kissing at the restaurant bar. This is how my father celebrated the happy news of my impending arrival, by destroying any sense of faithfulness to my mother. This very same woman swiftly became my dad's second wife. My mother endured the remaining months of her pregnancy alone, raising my toddler brother in a void of fatherly support.

My father never arrived at the hospital the day I was born, despite my birth being a scheduled c-section. He was already expecting a child with his new wife and we did not fit into his busy schedule. My dad had instructed my mom to name me Christine if I was a girl- a curious request given his absence from our family. Empowered by defiant independence, my mother choose a different name. She bestowed upon me her favorite nickname from college. There were so many Carols on her floor freshman year at SUNY Cortland, everyone started calling her "Carrie," and the name stuck.

I'm proud to be the bearer of my mother's name. It means "song of joy," which is pretty appropriate for both of us. However, I also know that my very name is a testament of my father's lack of interest in our lives. And that lack of interest left a gaping hole in my heart.

5. Babysitters and Bedtime

"When you go through deep waters, I will be with you." Isaiah 43:2

If I had known one tiny bit about the option of homeschooling when I was a child, I would have begged and begged my mom to instruct me in the safety of our home. Instead I feigned sickness at the slightest ache in my stomach or scratch in my throat. Being home sick with mom meant reading in bed, drinking Coke out of a bendy straw and maybe laying on the couch watching "The Price is Right." I loved being home. Even if it meant making myself sick with worry to stay there.

The only place in the world better than home was Nanny and Papa's house. That place was pure magic.

Nanny and Papa are my mom's parents. Our little family of three would stay with them religiously every Friday night. It was always the highlight of my week. We'd drive twenty minutes to their house after school and enjoy a home-cooked dinner all together around their big kitchen table. This is where I learned to say, "yes, please," and, "no, thank you," when I wanted someone to pass the carrots or did not want another serving of lima beans. These manners stuck with me right into the delivery room many years later where the nurses were sure I wasn't in active labor because I was being far too polite.

After dinner at Nanny and Papa's, Mom would head over to the Card Party or Bingo at the nearby community center with her friends. This was Mom's big night out and we all supported her getting a break. My older brother Charlie and I would watch The Donny and Marie Osmond Show with Nanny and Papa in the living room. We'd sing and dance and impersonate all the corny jokes. (Okay, this was mostly me. I was not shy at Nanny and Papa's house. I was the star singer, dancer and aspiring comedian.)

In the morning, Mom would sleep in while Charlie and I ate breakfast on metal TV trays, watching cartoons for hours. Apple Jacks, cinnamon toast, and orange juice would be neatly arranged on our matching trays. (I still buy Apple Jacks on days I miss my grandparents. This happens more often than you'd imagine for a woman with a mortgage and a minivan.)

My brother and I would cheer on the Road Runner as Wile E. Coyote would attempt using another failed ACME product to catch his nemesis.

Nanny and Papa had a treasure chest of goodies in their bedroom. It was a fancy clothes hamper full of prizes we could win for being well-behaved. Puzzles, jump ropes, jacks, coloring books. If we displayed excellent manners and listening skills during a visit, we might be rewarded with a new set of watercolor paints or a bottle of bubbles to take home with pride. That mystical hamper was a fabulous motivator.

Nanny and Papa were definitely my child care of choice, but they lived out of town so time with them was usually limited to weekends. My mom would sometimes need help on a weeknight so she could attend a PTA meeting or something else important and adult-like. This typically meant hiring Mrs. Hoskins from down the street. Mrs. Hoskins was in her 70's and did all of her kid management right from the living room couch.

Her advanced age and apparent immobility did not stop her from playing kickball with us. She would sit in her self-assigned position on the sofa where she played full-time pitcher and outfielder. She'd use a broom to retrieve the 3-inch foam ball from anyplace outside of her reach in our tiny living room. Charlie and I would run the bases, from the TV to the brown chair to the tweed couch to the coffee table and then back to the TV- all before Mrs. Hoskins threw you out- which was surprisingly often.

Having Mrs. Hoskins babysit was quite a treat because we were absolutely, under no uncertain terms, allowed to play ball in the house. And Mrs. Hoskins knew it. Old people make fantastic rebels! We never told, and Mom never knew. Kickball in the living room was 1,000 times better than gym class.

Then there was the night Mom couldn't get Mrs. Hoskins. Or Mrs. Price's pretty daughter. All of Weaver Street was letting my mother down. One of our neighbor's desperately offered her teenage son Brandon to babysit for us. Completely out of options, Mom finally took her up on the idea.

Brandon was a few years older than my brother. At the time he was maybe 14. The only distinct age marker I have comes from watching Charlie walk to school with Brandon the day after he babysat us. I was still in Elementary School, and they were headed to Middle School together. I remember thinking, "Don't walk to school with him Charlie! He's a bad person!"

I never had those thoughts about Brandon before. We were good friends with all of our neighbors. Brandon had often played catch in the yard with my brother, and he gave me my first cat, Tuffy years earlier. He had brown hair, was strong and always seemed older than his actual age.

When Mom couldn't secure Mrs. Hoskins that night, I remember being disappointed but pleasantly surprised at the thought of Brandon taking care of us. I bet he'd play kickball with us, and he'd even get off the couch.

We didn't play any kickball that night, but we did watch TV past our bedtime. Or at least Charlie got to. Brandon insisted I go to bed early. It was a school night, after all. He would tuck me in. Mrs. Hoskins never tucked me. She always stayed on the couch.

When my mom would tuck me in, she would sit on the edge of the bed, pull the covers up to my chin, kiss my cheek and wish me "sweet dreams." If I wasn't feeling well, or I was having a bad day, she might scratch my back for a while or even draw letters on my back, and I would have to guess what they were. I always loved that game. My husband still plays this game with me today because he's awesome.

He didn't want to play that game. Brandon had a different game in mind. When I climbed into bed, I was surprised that he climbed right into bed with me. He pulled the covers up over our heads like we were in a fort. "Want to play a game?" he asked.

"Yes!" I said enthusiastically. I've always loved games. I did not want to go to sleep.

"You touch my snake, and I'll touch your pussy," he said.

I was confused. My cat Tuffy was outside for the night. And I never knew Brandon had a snake. I had absolutely no idea what he was talking about.

He proceeded to grab my little hand and shove it down his pants. I remember feeling hair, and something hard, and thinking this was not a fun game at all.

I wanted Brandon to go home. I wanted Mrs. Hoskins to come back. I wanted Charlie to never talk to this boy again.

23

I don't know how long Brandon stayed in my bed that night. I just know I started crying any time my mom said he was coming to babysit.

My mom never knew about Brandon. At first I was too confused to explain it. By the time I understood, even a little, I was too embarrassed to tell anyone. When I was older, I didn't want to tell my mom because I didn't want her to feel guilty. It wasn't her fault she needed to have a teenage boy babysit me.

I blamed my dad. If he was there, we wouldn't need Brandon. And dads don't let terrible things happen to their little girls.

I always felt I was worthless after this happened. I became a victim, and there was no one who could rescue me. I believed I had no value worth protecting. My joy and innocence was lost. I became known as a kid who was often sad and withdrawn. It hadn't always been that way.

When I was in kindergarten, I owned a light blue denim pants suit with bright red and green apple trees printed all over it. It had the words "I like you," written over and over again in wavy white letters between the trees. It was the first sentence I learned to read or write, thanks to that most friendly outfit. I distinctly remember being so proud of my newfound ability to communicate this sentiment in written form. I would write "I like you" on little scraps of paper and happily distribute them to neighbors, classmates and family members.

Everyone was a friend just waiting to be discovered. My natural instinct upon meeting someone new was, "I like you!"

This was true until I was betrayed in the most personal way by someone I trusted. Someone I liked and I thought liked me back. My outgoing, friendly demeanor turned shy and reserved. I became fearful and silent, ashamed of a secret I didn't understand. A world was opened to me I knew I should not be a part of, but I knew no way of escape.

When you have your innocence stolen, something inside of you shatters. You no longer feel whole and pure. You feel dirty and guilty even though you've done nothing wrong. It filled me with fear and resentment. I felt ugly and broken. I stopped liking me.

My entire life I have hated the word pussy. When I hear it anywhere, it sends an eerie chill up my spine and fills me with anger. It immediately brings me back to my childhood bedroom where I felt vulnerable and afraid. It is a word meaning inferiority and worthlessness. It is dark and ugly and to this day makes my skin crawl.

There's a scene in the movie Forrest Gump where Forrest's best friend Jenny returns to her abandoned and dilapidated childhood home as an adult. She starts hurling rocks at it with all her might as she remembers the abuse she suffered there. In Forrest's voiceover narrative he states, "Sometimes there's just not enough rocks."

This is exactly how I felt.

I struggled for years to get the anger out. You have to face the truth to forgive it, and I wasn't able to do that easily. I didn't want to think about this happening to me. For years, I simply ignored it. I even tried to convince myself it wasn't true. But pretending or wishing it didn't happen does nothing to erase reality.

It wasn't until I was an adult and finally told my mother about Brandon that I began to feel free from the pain. She apologized, although I never saw it as her fault. I had no way to contact Brandon and tell him how he had hurt me. Somehow telling my mother and talking about it out loud with someone I love allowed me to begin the process of forgiving Brandon and freeing myself.

If only I had said something sooner. I wouldn't have spent so many years feeling worthless and afraid.

I'm not sure why so many of us keep this kind of abuse a secret. It's much more common that you realize, but you don't know that when it's happening to you. When you are the victim, you are certain you're only one. This terrible thing is *your* terrible thing. Too many of us have faced it all alone, too ashamed to tell another living soul.

6. Big Brother: *Julie's Story*

"Our past may shape us, but it doesn't define who we become." Alyson Noel

It started when she was very young.

Julie is not sure of the exact age she was when the abuse began. She just knows it happened a lot. Her older brother would sneak into her bedroom late at night. He'd climb into bed with her and touch her in ways no brother should touch his sister. She didn't understand what was happening. She just knew she didn't like it. She knew she wanted it to stop.

She feared going to bed at night. Sometimes she would pile up pillows in front of her bedroom door, hoping it would keep her brother from coming in. She dreaded it. When he did come in, she'd pretend to be asleep, hoping he would leave. But he didn't. The abuse went on for years.

Julie didn't know why it happened. She didn't know what she'd done wrong. She didn't know how to make it stop. Her brother threatened her, forcing her not to tell. Julie became his addiction.

As they got older, she was sure he knew better. She knew it was wrong and so did he. But he didn't stop. She was a prisoner in her own house. She never felt safe as long as he was home.

By the time she reached high school, she'd had enough. She was desperate to make it stop. They were on a family trip at Disney World when her parents left them alone in the hotel room. He insisted she take off all her clothes in front of him. For the first time ever, she stood up to him. She told him, "No! I'm too old for this. It has to stop!"

It stopped that night. Julie could not believe it. After years of suffering, she had finally found her voice.

Her new-found sense of victory quickly faded. Soon after they returned home from vacation, her brother snuck into her bedroom again. He abused her again. And again. And again. All the way through high school. It wasn't until Julie left for college that the sexual abuse stopped for good.

She blames herself for letting it go on for so long. It is *not* her fault.

Julie does not come from a single parent family. Or a poor family. Or a classically defined "dysfunctional" family. She comes from a healthy, middle class, family of faith. They pray together. Do devotions together. Go to church together.

These truths make it even more difficult for her to tell anyone what happened. I was the first and only person she ever told about the abuse. She wants to confront her brother, but has no idea how. She wants to tell her parents, but she's afraid they won't forgive him. She is certain it will crush them to know the truth about their son.

For years, she has lived in secret shame. She is sure there is something wrong with her. She has never had a boyfriend, and she's convinced she never will. She feels broken. Inadequate. How can anyone truly love her? How could she ever enjoy sex with a husband someday? She only associates it with emotional and physical pain.

I had these same questions. These same exact thoughts. And they haunted me for years.

7: Scary Carrie Sour

"And that's the thing about people who mean everything they say. They assume everyone else does too." Khalead Hosseini

My mom always said she received two good things from my dad: wonderful kids and a great last name. It's easy to make a good first impression with a name like Sweet. Especially in class when they take attendance last name first. I was always Sweet Carrie from the first day of school.

My first grade teacher was one of my favorites. She was always patient and kind. She was tall and thin with a classic 70's blonde bob. She often bent down to speak to you at eye level. And she taught me how to read. I'll never forget the woman who opened this magical door for me.

Near the end of the school year we were all making paper eagles to give to our dads on Father's Day. We cut out tiny white and yellow feathers and carefully glued them in rows onto brown construction paper. After painstakingly completing my eagle, I burst into tears because I had no father to bring my beautiful bird home to.

Immediately, my teacher noticed I was distraught over my purposeless project. She walked me to the principal's office with Kevin Brown, the only other kid in class with divorced parents. At first I was terrified we were in some kind of trouble. Instead, she presented our eagles to the principal. He accepted our offerings with enthusiasm and displayed them prominently on his office door for everyone to see.

I was so proud on that day. It was the first time I ever felt special for *not* having a dad.

Dads would come on the school field trips. Dads would take their kids trick or treating. Dads would push their daughters on the swings at the park. Dads would tell all the best jokes. But I didn't have a dad to do any of those things. Instead, it was always my mom. I didn't mind. My mom was really swell. I just wondered what I was missing.

Being the single parent of two young children made it hard for my mom to have a full-time job. She also found it more difficult to work after her brain surgery. Years later she would discover she qualified for disability insurance, but at the time, she didn't know this help was available. Dad provided no monetary support, leaving the financial burden of our family squarely on my mom.

This meant second-hand clothes, at-home haircuts, and cars that frequently broke down on the side of the road. While other girls at school were going to dance lessons and horseback riding, I was reading in my bedroom or climbing trees in the yard. Usually by myself.

I did not fit in well at school. Not only did I wear outdated clothes and read a lot, I was terribly shy. If someone didn't talk to me, I didn't talk to them. People find this hard to believe now. I'm a 9.8 out of 10 on the extrovert scale. (I always lose .2 points because I still love to read.) Today I will talk to anyone, anywhere about anything, but back then I was 98% introvert.

My favorite pastime at recess was swinging. It was the one thing a girl could do all by herself on the playground and not be bothered. Most girls would jump rope or play tag. The boys usually played kickball or climbed on the monkey bars. Sometimes the girls would chase the boys around the blacktop in large, obnoxious hoards. I would watch it all from high up on the swings and daydream about being anywhere else.

By third grade, other kids started teasing me. A lot. My shyness was compounded by being a bedwetter. I did not always smell the best at school. I avoided sitting close to other people, desperately hoping no one would notice. If I brushed up against a kid's desk as I walked by, they would pretend to spray it and say it was corroded. They called me "Scary Carrie" and "Carrie Sour." I never spoke up or defended myself. I just tried to ignore it. I couldn't wait to go home most days.

Being at home with my mom was safe. She would go out of her way to make sure I felt loved and secure. I once wet my pants in gym class at school. It was humiliating, and I never wanted to go back to gym again. My mom somehow got a doctor's note excusing me from gym class for the rest of the year.

The only thing I was ever good at in gym was running. I had lots of practice running away from bullies. And I would always make a beeline for the swings right after lunch. There were only four and if you didn't get there first, you weren't getting a swing at all! Most days I would run home from school because I could not get there fast enough. But otherwise, gym was deadly embarrassing. The shy kid is the last one picked for every team. It felt like that kid was always me.

"Sticks and stones may break my bones, but words will never hurt me." This is a mantra I grew up with as a kid. It was meant to give me confidence. Unfortunately, the complete opposite was true. Words are powerful to me. The teasing hurt a lot. The worst part is, I believed the mean things kids would say about me.

I was so impacted by the bullying, I lost confidence in my abilities and opinions.

Always seeking ways to help, my mom found a friend of my aunt to serve as a "big sister" for me. We would meet about once a month. Brenda would take me to the movies or out for ice cream. One of my favorite outings was a trip to the Danbury Fair. It was extraordinary! We rode rides and watched shows and ate candied apples on wooden sticks. All day long I chattered away excitedly, sharing opinions and ideas about all sorts of things. At the end of the day, my big sister Brenda shared an observation.

"Carrie," she said, "I notice you start every sentence with 'My mom thinks....' or "Charlie always says...' or 'My teacher told me...' but I want to know what you think. What do you have to say? What do you believe? You need to learn to think for yourself."

I had no idea how to respond. I had nothing to say. My opinions didn't matter. I didn't trust my own ideas. I didn't dare share my own thoughts. I assumed everyone thought I was a loser.

It was far too long before this way of thinking ever changed for me. The hurtful words of others stripped me of my sense of self. Too often we allow ourselves to believe the lies people tell us. We begin to repeat these lies to ourselves. The truth is, we have the freedom to decide who we are and who we want to become.

The careless words of others spoken out of spite, jealousy or their own insecurity should have no bearing on our identity. There will always be people who criticize and condemn out of ignorance. Don't give them any power by believing what they say. You know the truth about who you are and who you'd like to be. It's time to speak it.

You have incredible value and worth.

8. Shields Up: *Veronica's Story*
(In her own words)

"You wear a mask for so long, you forget who you were beneath it." Alan Moore

No one likes middle school. For me, it was my own personal hell. Those years are hard enough for everyone, but if you were an overweight, shy, frizzy-haired girl who loved reading, science, and the Beatles, the odds were stacked against you. It didn't help that I was the teacher's-pet type who took pride in going above and beyond on assignments as well as answering questions in class. It was no surprise that I was an easy target.

There was some typical name-calling, one of my books ended up with "loser" written on the front, and one time somebody colored in the numbers on my locker combination lock, but over time, the situation started to get worse and more personal.

There was a boy in my sixth-grade homeroom whose desk was across from mine, and he made it his mission to bother me as often as he could. Greg would mock me when I answered questions, read my assignments out loud when we had to switch papers, and repeatedly asked me out and told me he loved me. The latter would occur multiple times per day, and eventually a few others joined in. It could be in the hallway, the library, in classrooms, or just about anywhere imaginable at school. I felt as if I couldn't go anywhere without one of them finding me.

I would go to my parents and teachers and tell them what happened, but it never helped. My parents, although well-intentioned, only gave me cliche statements such as, "Just ignore them," "They're just jealous of you," or, my least favorite, "He's only doing this because he likes you." I tried ignoring him, but that just led to more bullying and being called much worse names than "nerd" or "geek." Eventually, I gave up asking for help and resolved to handle things on my own.

I quickly learned to use a few defense mechanisms to my advantage, often hiding behind sarcasm and self-deprecating humor. Sometimes if I brought myself down first, the bullies would be satisfied and go away. When classmates would make fun of me because I was smart and liked to use big words, I would make sure I threw a few of those words into my response - an act of defiance to show them that they weren't getting to me, even though internally I felt hurt.

But there was always more to face each day as middle school went on. It seemed that the favorite subject of the bullies was the fact that I liked to read. I carried a book everywhere and would often be found reading when I had finished an assignment early, in the cafeteria, or in the few minutes before class started. It gave me something to focus on instead of making eye contact or dejectedly staring at the floor.

One time they grabbed my book and threw it into the trash. There was a day when I was reading during lunch and one girl pulled out a camera and started taking pictures of me. I repeatedly told her to stop and did my best to ignore her and hide my face from the camera, but rumor had it that the pictures ended up on MySpace.

Then it would get physical. I never really liked to be touched, or to hug people, and somehow that information became known to the large group of kids who would use it against me. In gym class, there was a girl who would grab or pinch me, smirk, and run away. A boy in another class would punch and jab at me when the teacher wasn't looking. Others would sit down next to me and put their arm around me, laughing when I flinched or shook them off. Then there was another guy, who one day in study hall came out of nowhere and bear-hugged me. I instinctively flailed to get away, almost knocking over a chair in the process.

What would happen at school would seep into my home life. I had a short temper with my family, became more introverted than normal, and when my family would make innocent jokes with me, I would get upset because it reminded me of school. Sometimes my relatives would make fun of me for getting upset with their jokes, forcing me to re-live the mocking I endured at school.

I had to learn to put my shields up and hide my emotions, in order to not show that I was upset. I learned to endure the teasing and not let myself cry, to keep my voice steady when I responded to questions, and to not make eye contact with whoever was terrorizing me that day. I also learned not to show excitement for things I enjoyed, lest my classmates pick on me because I was happy about an activity, an interesting fact, or anything else they felt worth using against me.

I felt that I couldn't trust anyone, and if someone was nice to me for no particular reason, I suspected ulterior motives. Years later I stamped out potential friendships with my silence, sarcastic retorts, or brutal candor. The guilt remained long after - I was only trying to protect myself but unintentionally struck out against and possibly hurt others. At the time, I thought it was better to be safe than sorry, but once it was okay to come out from behind the shields, I felt shame.

The worst incident of all came at the end of eighth grade. It was a day I had been looking forward to for months-- the grade-wide field trip to a science museum. I couldn't wait, but when the day arrived, it was less than perfect. I ended up exploring the museum all by myself. It wasn't all that bad until I got on the bus to come back to the school.

I was sitting quietly, reading the book I had brought for the two-hour ride. The girls behind me starting teasing me. First they picked on my nerdy science book. Then my appearance. Then, one of them reached forward and ran a brush through my untamable hair. That was the last straw, and I told them to stop. They did for a little while, but then something worse happened.

Another girl started a rumor that I had had sex with a boy from one of my classes. It began to circulate through the whole bus. I was mortified. Not only did I barely know the guy in question, but I was a naive 13 year-old who had never even thought about sex. I looked out the window and tried not to draw any further attention. I tried to convince myself that I was misinterpreting things - that they were talking about someone else and not me, but then a voice rang out from the back of the bus, loud enough for everyone to hear.

"Hey Veronica! Did you use protection?"

Yeah, they were definitely talking about me, and I did not want to go down without a fight. However, retaliating now wouldn't help me. *Shields up, Veronica. Don't let them see you get upset.*

When I got home that day I told my parents, who in turn told the assistant principal. A few days later I was called down to her office, where she asked me to tell her what happened. She promised I was safe and my name wouldn't be revealed to anyone. The primary bully from that day put two and two together. Barely a few hours after I'd left the principal's office, I was walking down the hallway and heard her say, "So I got called down to the office today because of Veronica!" Then she saw me and immediately turned to her friends. "Hey, did you hear Veronica's going out with Mike?"

Okay, "going out" wasn't as bad as the sex rumor, but I wasn't thrilled rumors were still going around. Clearly whatever the assistant principal said hadn't deterred my classmates one bit. Still, I walked by and tried to ignore them.

'Shields up. They don't need to know you heard them. Don't look them in they eye and keep moving. You'll be safe when you get to your desk and the teacher is watching...

I was all too familiar with that internal monologue,

The results of this bullying sent out waves that would follow me for years. I had the hardest time trusting people, accepting a compliment, or being open with people because somewhere inside I was afraid to let my guard down. It wasn't always a conscious choice, but my shields stayed up long after the time I needed them had passed. It made me even more of an introvert and it hardened my heart. It was a long time before I could even begin to chip away at the walls I built around me - I had built them well.

Guilt and shame followed me as well. Somewhere along the way I got the idea that the things that had happened to me were my fault. I thought that maybe, if I had just changed, if I had just conformed, if I had stopped doing some of the things I liked, then maybe those kids would have left me alone. Maybe I should have just cut my losses and given in.

It took almost a decade to finally look back and accept that no, there was nothing I could have done. If I had tried to change for them, they would have likely found something else to target.

No matter the pain, frustration, or residual shame, there is one thing I am sure of: I won. I, the ultimate loser in they eyes of my classmates, emerged victorious. But it's not because of what I've accomplished since then or perhaps that I turned out "better." I have no idea what those people are doing these days, and it's not really any of my business. o how do I know that I won?

My classmates could strip me of my pride, my dignity, and my confidence. They could make me afraid to go to school each day, make me question what I had done to deserve my misery, and hate myself for the situation I had found myself in. However, there were some things that were out of their reach, and they were the important ones.

They couldn't make me stop reading, no matter how much they interrogated me while doing so. They couldn't silence me in my favorite classes, even though they mocked me when I gave correct answers. They couldn't keep me from listening to my "unpopular" music, make me wear "trendy" clothes, or quash my love for learning new "nerdy" trivia and facts. My walls and my defenses were not infallible, but they protected the things I valued and what made me the individual I was proud to be. To this day I still love to read, dress how I like, and watch Jeopardy almost every night.

As much as they tried, my peers could not reduce me to anything less than my true self. I won.

And years later, the shields are finally coming down.

9. Please Don't Kick Me

"Nothing haunts us like the things we don't say." Mitch Albom

Veronica's story is so similar to mine, it's painful for me to read her words. Life definitely got worse for me in middle school. Sixth grade was an absolute nightmare. This was the year that the five elementary schools in our area would combine. I was hoping for a fresh start. What I got were new enemies and more bullying.

Science class was the worst. The teacher was ancient, making him hard-of-hearing and practically blind. Kids always acted out in his class because they knew they could get away with just about anything.

Being picked on for years actually made me compassionate toward others. At home I was taught to be a safe person, and I knew others needed a safe place. I wasn't the only one teased in school. I was always aware of the kid who was picked on and excluded. My teachers would often seat new kids next to me because they knew I'd make them feel welcome.

Teachers also knew I was well-behaved and compliant. I was often placed as a diffuser between two trouble makers. I didn't mind sitting next to a new kid, but being the buffer zone between a couple of bad kids never ended well for me.

In science class, there weren't just two trouble makers but six. All boys. And they all sat in the back of the classroom. They infuriated our teacher. He would get so mad at them, he would make a fist with his hand and repeatedly bang his gold ring with a large red stone loudly onto the desk. Not just any desk but my desk- every time!

I sat in the front row, right in front of the teacher's desk. This was always my preferred seat. It was usually the safest place to be. Except in 6th grade science class. I cringed every time my teacher lost his temper, knowing that giant ring was going to come crashing down on my desk with a deafening blow.

When he finally moved me to a new seat near the back of the room, I was relieved. For about three minutes. That's when I realized I'd been taken out of the frying pan and tossed directly into the fire.

I was surrounded by trouble makers. The boys on either side of me talked about me to each other throughout the whole class period. Making comments about my face, my clothes, my hair, and it only got worse from there. I would try to ignore them. Keep my eyes forward and try to learn something about science without crying.

After our weekly quizzes, we had to trade papers with the person next to us. Mine always came back with terrible things written on them. Mean words written about me in pen I could not erase. I never turned these quizzes in because I was too ashamed of what they said. I'd take zeros to avoid the embarrassment.

The worst bully of all sat directly behind me. It started with him kicking my chair. Then pulling my hair. One time, I was returning to my seat after turning in an assignment. He pulled my chair out from under me with his foot, and I fell to the ground, hard. I was so embarrassed, I wanted to run straight out of the classroom.

I didn't know how to laugh at myself then. I didn't know how to push back. I didn't know the cleverness of sarcasm and the magic of self-confidence. Oh how I wish the person I am now could go back to sixth grade and stand up to that motley crew of prepubescent boys!

Instead, I suffered in silence. One time the kid in the seat behind me managed to put a "Kick Me" sign on my back. I don't know how long I walked around with that stupid sign on me, but I remember bending over to get something out of my locker when someone actually kicked me! I stood up straight, shocked, and looked at the kid incredulously. He shrugged his shoulders and said, "The sign on your back says 'Kick Me,' so I did." And then he casually walked away. I was livid. How could somebody do that to me? Why would anyone be so mean? I was never mean to anyone. I didn't deserve this! I ripped the sign off my back and slammed my locker shut.

The next day in science class, all the boys in the back were snickering as I walked to my seat. "Carrie, why would you want people to kick you? Who puts a "Kick Me" sign on their back? You're so weird."

I wanted to yell at them. I wanted to scream saying I knew it was them and they were a bunch of jerks! I was so angry. But I didn't have that kind of courage. I didn't realize when you like yourself, others like you too. When you're confident, others don't find it fun to mess with you. When you're shaking in your no-name brand sneakers, terrified someone will say one more mean thing to you, someone says one more mean thing to you.

And that's exactly what they did. I started staying home sick to avoid science class. I missed over forty days of school in sixth grade. Between absences, not turning in quizzes, and being distracted in class, I got my first D on my report card. I wanted to die. I remember hiding behind my bedroom door crying because I was ashamed to have performed so poorly. I didn't want my mom to know.

I couldn't believe what happened when she finally found me on that awful report card day. She wasn't angry. She didn't yell. She asked me what was happening in science class. She listened, and she believed me. And she took me straight to school to talk to the teacher.

He had no idea. It was clear he regretted his decision to send me to the back of the room. I was returned to my previous seat at the front of the class. Two of those bullying boys landed in detention. Another soon received long term suspension from school. Now that my teacher was aware of what was happening in his classroom, he was enabled to act and provided just consequences.

My grades improved, and I gained a bit of confidence. I had been heard by my mother and my teacher, and my words had been valued. If only I'd trusted my mom and spoken up sooner. Maybe I could have avoided all of that teasing.

It's a risk to speak up, to tell the truth about the hard things you've suffered. It's embarrassing, even humiliating to admit you've been taken advantage of. You may not be heard or even believed at first but, if you find the right person, you can get the help you need. It's important to have your feelings validated by someone who cares about you.

Your voice grows stronger each time you find the courage to use it.

10. Flirting With Danger

"Forgive yourself for the decisions you have made, the ones you still call mistakes when you tuck them in at night." Sarah Kay

By seventh grade all of my friends were obsessed with "development." All the girls could not wait to get their period and need a bra. I had experienced both of these milestones in late elementary school and was mortified by it all. There is nothing more embarrassing than having your male gym teacher tell your mother she needs to buy you a bra because you're bouncing all over gym class. As if gym weren't humiliating enough!

By middle school, guys started beeping their horns and yelling out their car windows at me when I would walk down the street. It was embarrassing and made me feel uncomfortable. I learned to walk with my shoulders hunched, trying to hide myself.

About this same time, a childhood friend of my mother's offered to pay for my brother and me to have braces. He knew she could not afford it, and he wanted to help. Charlie's teeth were worse than mine. He had problems with his jaw and required surgery in addition to braces. Mom's friend not only provided the braces for both of us, he flew my mom and brother to Arizona where he lived so Charlie could have the necessary surgery.

I remember Dad stopping by for one of his rare, surprise visits soon after Charlie had his surgery. Mine weren't due to go on for a few weeks. Mom was worried that dad would ask how we had paid for the braces. He knew she couldn't afford it. She didn't want Dad to be angry. Looking back now, I'm not sure what we were afraid he would do. I just remember being terrified of him finding out.

When Dad arrived, Charlie hid in the basement. After a few hours went by, it was clear, Dad wasn't going home anytime soon. He'd been drinking and was especially sociable. Mom and I couldn't get him to leave. As time went by, I became more and more nervous. We had to get my brother and his braces out of the house.

I sat by my open bedroom window, crying, feeling helpless. I must have been audibly sobbing because our neighbor heard me as he walked by. He called out to me, asking if I was okay. He was a dad who made me feel safe. I told him what was happening. He told me to send Charlie out my window and over to their house. My dad would not find him there, and his braces would remain a secret.

My bedroom was at the end of the hall, right across from the basement stairs of our ranch-style house. We made a plan for Charlie to silently creep across the hall to my room where he would jump out of my first floor window and run over to the neighbor's house.

Before we mustered the courage to implement this plan, my father abruptly left. Our neighbor had come over and asked him to leave. Our dad did not make any other surprise visits during the three years my brother and I had our teeth in prison.

Not only did those braces provide me with a smile I could be proud of, I had experienced generosity from a man I barely knew. This was incredible to me. It gave me a renewed sense of hope. Maybe I was more valuable and worthy of love than I thought.

About this same time, my mom took me to get my first professional hair cut. With my newly straightened teeth, television-worthy hair and excessive eighties eyeliner, life was starting to change for me. Babysitting jobs allowed me to buy some new clothes. I finally looked like everyone else, and it was easier to make friends. I enjoyed fitting in for what felt like the first time in my life.

I was invited to new friends' houses. I enjoyed school dances. I even tried smoking behind the bathrooms at the town fair. I hated it. Both smoking and drinking never held much appeal for me. They were my dad's bad habits, and I didn't want them to become mine. Drinking especially seemed like sleeping with the enemy. I never wanted to be like my father, dependent on "liquid courage," as he called it.

But I loved hanging out with my new, cool friends. We'd all get dressed up, spending hours on our hair and make-up. We'd beg our moms to drop us off at the mall for the afternoon or evening. After several trips to the mall, we noticed guys started following us. This became a foolish game we'd play. We'd walk into random stores and see if they'd follow us. If they continued to hang around after several stores, we'd have the bravery to talk to them.

My new friends were pretty. Really pretty. And confident. They didn't seem to be afraid of anything, and I liked that. I was afraid of everything and wanted to be more like them.

My friend Brooke would always initiate the conversation with guys. As the prettiest one, she'd always get the cutest guy. As the second prettiest, Jessie would get the second best looking guy. Then there was me. I was always the one with the "great personality." This typically meant I ended up with the least attractive person who hopefully had a good sense of humor and some manners.

Our first several times meeting guys at the mall, this little game usually resulted in some free ice cream at Friendly's or maybe even a movie at the cinema next door. It seemed pretty innocent and harmless. Over time, it evolved into drinking rum and Coke in mall parking lots and making out in cars with perfect strangers. I always hated this part. I'd try to make excuses not to head to the parking lot. Sometimes I'd find a payphone and ask my mom to come pick me up. Other times I'd end up holding an empty beer can while making lame jokes, trying to fit in while staying out of some guy's back seat. Everything about this was uncomfortable.

One Saturday night we were foolish enough to climb into a car with a bunch of guys and ended up at this random house. These boys were older, and it made me nervous. I knew this was a stupid decision, but I hadn't backed out soon enough. As they led us into the dark, empty house, the messy kitchen contained only junk food, and there were beer cans and Capri Sun littered around. There were no signs of responsible adults living in this place.

All too quickly, my friends disappeared with their guys. "We'd better pick a bedroom before we get left with the couch," 3rd ranked guy joked as he took me by the hand and started leading me down a hallway.

Bedroom? I don't need a bedroom. No, thank you. Where's the car? I'm ready to go home. These were the thoughts in my head. But I didn't say them out loud. As usual. The guy wrapped his arms around my waist and started kissing me, pushing me toward the bedroom door. Brooke and Jessie were nowhere in sight. They must have gone into other bedrooms. "It's alright," he said. " You're safe here. You can stay as long as you want."

Stay? I had no interest in staying. I didn't even want to be here.

I felt trapped. I had no way to get home. I couldn't call my mom to come get me because I didn't even know where I was. How could I be so stupid?

Maybe this wasn't terrible. Maybe I should just do what I assume my friends had done. Maybe it wouldn't be absolutely awful. Did it really matter anyway? Did I even have a choice?

When you suffer from sexual abuse as a child you feel broken. Once you're damaged, you no longer believe your personal privacy can be protected. You develop a warped sexual identity. I'd never had sex before, but Brandon had introduced me to sexual activity as a kid. It piqued a curiosity that I did not understand.

In seventh grade, I found several Playboy and Playgirl magazines at the neighbor's house while babysitting. I knew I shouldn't look at them but I did. I'd put the kids to bed and lock myself in the parents' bedroom with those magazines for hours. I was sure something was wrong with me. Why was I interested in sex when I hated it? Why would I even want someone to touch my body when I was ashamed of it?

I finally gave in and let him lead me into the bedroom. As he shut the door behind us, I tried to combat feelings of fear. Maybe he just wants to kiss me more, I thought. Or maybe we'll just fool around like my friends had done so many times in the backseat of strangers' cars in the mall parking lot. When it was clear he did not just want to kiss me, my mind immediately thought, "NO!" but my voice said nothing.

I've been embarrassed about this decision my entire life, I actually wrote a fake paragraph about it, right up there where the true paragraph is. I told a courageous story of pushing the guy away, rushing into the bathroom and hoisting myself out the window. Then I bravely navigate my way home in the dark, tears streaming down my cheeks.

I wish it were true. After writing my dreamed up story, deleting it, and then writing what actually happened, I went upstairs and told my husband Erv this story for the very first time. After twenty years of marriage, he had never heard it. He knew he hadn't married a virgin. He didn't know I was thirteen, with a stranger, in a house that, for all I know, was used for sex trafficking. How could I allow that to happen? For years I tried to simply forget about it. I didn't know how to even begin talking about it.

After I told my husband, the shame slowly lost its power on me. As I mentioned the age 13, it struck me, we have a son who is thirteen. We build forts out of blankets together. We dig tunnels in the snow. We shoot rubber bands at each other. A few weeks ago, he memorized the first 118 digits of pi and won a pie at school. He brought it home for me in his backpack.

"You have a pie in your backpack?" I asked him.

"Yep! It's apple. You like apple, right Mom?"

"Um, yes. But honey, pies need to be kept horizontal. Pies don't do vertical," I told him.

"This one does." And then my sweet boy gave me a pile of pie.

That's how a thirteen year old thinks.

I'm so thankful I made it out of that house. Not all thirteen year old girls do. Sex traffickers prey on young girls who feel abandoned and worthless. They give you attention. Tell you you're beautiful, desirable. Tell you they'll take care of you. You can have ice cream and Capri Sun or beer if you want and it's okay. They promise you new clothes and a new life and for many girls it's temptation they can't resist.

I didn't once consider staying at that house. I loved my mom and my brother and I never wanted to leave them. But I longed for attention from a man. That's how so many teens and college students who have confided in me feel. When Dad is absent, it leaves a void. You desperately try to fill it. And often, that means putting yourself in danger. For some girls, they don't know what they've gotten into until it's too late.

The next day I felt dirty, used and broken. I wanted to restart my life. My past needed to be erased. I tore my posters of Rob Lowe and Tom Cruise off my walls. I threw out all my short skirts and crop tops. I stopped listening to Madonna. I focused on my school work and tried to make myself into a better person. The person my mom and my family had taught me to be. Someone who didn't make mistakes. Someone who could earn a prize from Nanny and Papa's magic hamper. Someone worthy of love.

11. Pool Party

"It takes ten times as long to put yourself back together as it does to fall apart." Suzanne Collins

By the following summer, I had moved on. No more sneaking around behind my mother's back. No more making up lies about where I was going and who I was going to be with. No more trying to get attention from boys. I was a new person, as long as no one knew the truth. And I would never tell them.

Before school started back up, my friend Jamie invited me to her house for a party. She was one of my few friends from elementary school, and I was happy to be invited. There were cousins, grandparents, aunts and uncles there. I had just lost my grandmother, Nanny, a few years earlier and I missed her terribly. It was comforting to be included in a family event. I sat in a lawn chair amidst the adults chatting about our big plans for high school. Freshman year was the perfect time for a fresh start. I couldn't wait to leave middle school and the bad memories behind.

The day was a scorcher, so we spent hours in the pool. We played Marco Polo and volleyball and perfected the art of flipping underwater. We'd take breaks to eat hot dogs and chips and soda. Jamie's family was generous. This was the kind of fun I wanted to have. I didn't need rum and Coke in a mall parking lot.

My friend's dad gave us rides around the pool. He would hold us around the waist and pull us around in the water, spinning us in circles. A bunch of us kids would create a long chain of bodies, holding on to each other, gliding along as he tugged us around the swimming pool.

As the day wore on, extended family members headed home. Jamie's grandparents wished me well in the new school year, encouraging me to try out for the school musical. Her aunt and uncle thought I'd make a great addition to the student council. I did not want this day of summer fun to end.

Fortunately, I was sleeping over so the party would extend into the night. After making gigantic ice cream sundaes, Jamie and I decided to go night swimming. We didn't even wait 30 minutes after dessert. We felt like true rebels risking a severe post-sundae cramp in the pool.

We jumped in just as Jamie's dad came out onto the deck. He placed his half empty beer can on the wooden pool railing and climbed down the ladder into the water. He offered to give us rides around in the pool just like he had in the afternoon. We started out in a chain of three, laughing and squealing as he whirled us around in the moonlight.

We chatted and joked about the day. Her dad was especially talkative and friendly. I'd never seen him this animated before. I felt so comfortable and at home. It was nice being with a dad. Jamie was lucky, and I was thankful she was sharing her father with me.

After a long period of "chain gliding," Jamie's dad offered us turns one at a time. First my friend, then me. When it was my turn, he put his hands around my waist. He invited me to lean my head back against his chest as he pulled me around the perimeter of the long, oval pool.

This was a strange feeling, reclining back on a man's chest. I'd seen Jamie do the same thing with her dad moments earlier. It was new to me. At first it was awkward, but then it was comforting. So this is what it feels like to really have a father?

It was so relaxing, I almost fell asleep.

Suddenly, I snapped awake, acutely aware of Jamie's dad's hands. They had started meandering, first across my stomach and then up to my chest. My mind started racing. What do I do? Why is he doing this? Is it an accident? It didn't feel like an accident. I said nothing but started to stiffen in his arms. He whispered in my ear, "It's okay. Just relax."

I was not relaxed. I was not going to relax. This was not okay at all. I reached for his arms and redirected his hands to my waist. How could that have just happened? This was Jamie's dad. Surely he didn't mean anything by it. I tried to stay calm and not worry. I was so good at worrying.

I had become well acquainted with bad things happening to me. It felt as if I was marked for abuse. Did people know they could get away with taking advantage of me? Was it obvious that I was unwilling or unable to defend myself? This put me in a constant state of anxiety, always expecting the worst.

Jamie got bored swimming by herself and headed for the ladder. "It's getting cold. I'm going inside."

"Go ahead honey,and help your mother clean up the kitchen," her dad instructed.

I wanted to leave with Jamie, but he tightened his grip around me. "What's your hurry? Aren't you having fun? Now we can be alone."

I was not having fun. I was starting to get scared. What did this guy want? I wanted to get away, but what if I was wrong? My family always taught me to respect adults. To trust grown-ups. I knew this man. He was my friend's father. I tried to relax. This was supposed to be fun.

His hands started to wander again, but this time they were moving toward my bikini bottoms. I started to stiffen again, holding my legs as tightly together as possible. "Relax, it's okay," he kept saying as his hands kept moving.

Why was this happening again? What was wrong with me? Maybe he'll stop. It'll all stop soon. I tried to think of a polite way to get out of that pool. Why does Sweet Carrie always have to be polite? Why can't she just speak her mind and say no?

It didn't stop. He persisted, his hands all over me. He whispered in my ear, the scent of beer strongly on his breath, "Spread your legs, you sexy little thing."

I could not let this happen again. I wouldn't. I kicked my legs hard against the side of the pool and broke away from Jamie's dad. I swam to the ladder as quickly as I could and ran into the house.

Shaking and scared, I told Jamie what happened. I was not staying silent this time. She immediately told her mom. A few minutes later, her mom came into Jamie's bedroom where I sat shivering on the bed wrapped in a towel, my hair still dripping wet from the pool.

"You must have misunderstood," her mom explained very calmly. "He was only joking. Just playing around. He would never hurt you."

I found my courage and repeated the words he had said. Words that I felt were clear and easy to interpret. "What else could, 'Spread your legs, you sexy little thing,' mean?" I asked, trying to be respectful yet insistent on revealing the truth.

Jamie's mom quickly left the room, flustered.

Several minutes later, her dad came in. My eyes met the floor as he sat down on the bed. "I'm sorry you're upset." he said. "I was just kidding. Don't you know a joke when you hear one? Where's your sense of humor?" He chuckled, trying to be charming. Hoping we would laugh. We did not laugh. Jamie and I both sat in bewildered silence.

Then he got very serious and stared at me, his eyes threatening. "I don't think you should mention this to your mom. She might not let you come over here anymore. You don't want that to happen, do you?"

I did not. I loved coming to Jamie's house. She was one of my best friends.

But I was tired of staying silent. I was tired of keeping shameful secrets. Why should I blame myself when I'd done nothing wrong?

I spent the night in Jamie's room, went home in the morning and, this time, immediately told my mom what happened. And she believed me.

I decided all fathers are jerks.

It would be some time before I would trust a man again. I felt so betrayed by a father-figure I trusted. This was a grown man with children. The parent of a friend. He wasn't a curious teenager who didn't know any better. He knew me and valued me and then reduced me to a piece of meat. At least, that's what it felt like. I had been treated like an object instead of a person. Again.

It wasn't until several years later when I discovered how incredible fathers could be. They can provide so much security and strength when they are loving and faithful. I see the impact of my husband's adoration on my own teenage girls. They have more confidence than I ever possessed when I was their age. They speak their minds and skillfully defend themselves. Their father's love infuses them with courage.

As a married woman, I now have a father-in-law who loves me like his own. He notices little things that are important to me. He cares for me when I'm sick or sad or hurting. He puts my needs before his own, even when it's inconvenient for him. I now know for certain not all fathers are selfish men.

When I was thirteen, I didn't understand the power of addiction. It leads people to make bad decisions. I'm sure once my friend's father was sober, he was ashamed of what he'd done. In time, I chose to forgive him. It wasn't easy, but I wouldn't allow his addiction to end my friendship with his daughter. His use of "liquid courage" gave him boldness to act in a shameful way. This does not excuse his actions, but it does fill me with pity toward him. I can move on and know that this will not define my life.

I do still want to punch him in the face.

Forgiveness. It's a process.

12. Daddy's Favorite: *Marla's Story*

"Even when I hear nothing, I rest in knowing He hears me." Bryce Avary

Maria loved her father. Growing up she would often go to work with him all day on Sundays. She enjoyed meeting his clients and coworkers. On those days her father was fun, sociable and outgoing. He was pleasant to be around.

Maria felt differently about her father at night. She always feared her father coming home at the end of a long day. She'd lay in bed praying he wouldn't open her bedroom door. She'd hope he was too tired to bother with her. She desperately prayed he would just go to sleep.

But he often wouldn't. The later he came home and the more he'd been drinking, the more likely he'd come into her bedroom. She doesn't know how old she was when her father began sexually abusing her, she just knows she was very young and didn't understand at first what was going on.

She'd secretly hope her mother would come in and find them together. Perhaps her mom would wonder where her father was and what he was doing. Her mother never came looking for her dad. If she did, she never stopped the abuse from happening.

She thought about locking her door, trying somehow to keep him out. But she knew he'd get angry and then things would be even worse. She never considered defending herself or telling anyone. She was too afraid of what he might do. He was angry and abusive. She was too scared to speak.

Over time, her dad became more bold. They'd be sitting in the living room watching television as a family. Maria's father would spread a blanket across their laps on the couch. He'd cuddle close to her, looking like a caring father. Then he'd put his hand down her pants and start touching her. Her mother and siblings would be right there in the same room. She would sit in silence, enduring the discomfort and shame. If anyone knew, they never dared say anything.

The abuse went on for years and years. All the way up through high school, when she was regularly being raped by her own father.

As she grew older he became protective and controlling of Maria. She wasn't allowed to have a boyfriend or wear clothing he felt showed off her figure. He always kept her close to him. She was his favorite, and it was awful.

He even chose where she went to college. The school was close to her home, but at last she would finally be out of that house and away from her father's abuse. He couldn't touch her anymore, emotionally or physically.

Eventually, he abandoned Maria's family. She didn't see or hear from him for years.

She graduated from college, got married and began a career. She never told her mother or her siblings about the abuse.

When her father reached out to her as an adult, he made an attempt to apologize for what he had done. Recognizing his struggle to get the words out, Maria told him she forgave him. She was tired of being angry. She wanted to move on. This was her chance to put it all behind her. He didn't have power over her anymore. She was finally free.

After years of marriage, she told her husband about the abuse. She didn't go into detail. Her husband wasn't sure how to handle it. She wanted him to know why she was sometimes uncomfortable with sex, but it was so hard to explain.

Maria doesn't want her past to be a barrier to her present. She's forgiven her dad and tries to move on, but that doesn't mean the memories have left her. Sometimes her husband will touch her a certain way, and it will trigger a memory. It turns her off and makes her unable to enjoy herself. She wants to fix this but doesn't know how.

She feels alone in her shame. She wonders if she's the only one? She wants to ask her sisters if they were abused. She wants to talk to her mom about it, but where does she begin? How does she possibly bring it up? Her family has suffered enough. She remains silent.

Sometimes our pain does define us. Time may lessen its grip, but the ongoing hold still lingers. It can show up just when we thought we were out of it's grasp.

13. First Love

"Be careful of love. It'll twist your brain around and leave you thinking up is down and right is wrong." Rick Riordan

I never really wanted to have sex. I was curious about it, but I wasn't really interested. It sounded kinda scary. My experience at that house in 8th grade was awful, and I didn't want anything more to do with it.

What I did want was a boyfriend. Someone to love me all the time. Someone I could trust. Someone like the boys in all the Judy Blume books I'd read. Young adult fiction had shaped my adolescent mind, and I believed Mr. Wonderful was real.

I found him in the cafeteria my freshmen year of high school.

My friend Kevin introduced us. "Carrie, this is Alex. He's a junior. He lives down the street from me."

"You're a junior? My brother is a junior! " I exclaimed. "Do you know my brother, Charlie Sweet?"

"Yeah, I do. We're friends. He's cool." Alex replied.

"I'm his sister!" I said excitedly.

"Wait! You're your brother's sister? No way!" Alex sarcastically replied.

I have always been super smooth under pressure.

It wasn't impressive, but it was a beginning. The beginning of many lunches and letters and a homecoming dance that turned into officially dating.

I didn't know it at the time, but Alex was the father figure I'd always wanted.

Alex worked in the record department at a local store. I thought it was the coolest job ever! Sometimes I'd spend hours at his work, visiting with him and helping alphabetize the new albums. We loved being the first to hear new music. He was a heavy metal fan like my brother. I was more of a Huey Lewis and the News kinda girl.

Alex was always generous. He spoiled me the way I always wanted my dad to. He bought me clothes and jewelery and Lucky Charms, my most favorite cereal. I got a dozen roses for Valentine's Day. Alex was stable and predictable and my family loved him.

My new boyfriend also had a car. This was fantastic because we could go to the movies. Go to the fair. Go to the park. He drove me to school. He drove me home from school. He drove me everywhere I wanted to go. I had my own personal chauffeur.

We also parked that car. A lot. Alongside dirt roads and behind creepy cemeteries late at night. I never wanted to go too far, but I always wanted to make Alex happy. I hated telling him "no." Silent Sweet Carrie strikes again.

After dating for about six months, I found a note from Alex crammed into my locker. He referenced the movie we had seen the weekend before. It was a corny, teenage movie where a very young Jim Carey has to lose his virginity to avoid becoming a vampire. Or to become a vampire. I honestly can't remember which. Either way, he and some girl end up having sex in a coffin. Alex's note asked if we could do the same thing they did, without the coffin.

I did not know what to say. We'd been dating for what seemed like an extremely long time. Our friends were surprised we weren't already having sex. I wasn't interested, but he definitely was.

We loved each other. I was sure of that. And we'd talked about getting married after high school and college. We even had a date picked out- the anniversary of the homecoming dance where we became boyfriend and girlfriend.

I couldn't think of a good reason to say no, other than I didn't want to and I was afraid of getting pregnant. So I stalled. I needed to be responsible and go to Planned Parenthood to get some birth control like I had heard other girls at school do. I managed to postpone the "coffin thing," as we often called it, for months.

I was uncomfortable and afraid, but sex eventually became a part of our dating life. I gave in to the pressure of believing this was what you did if you loved someone. And I loved Alex. I didn't want to lose him.

Sometimes we have the wrong idea about love. Love is not self-seeking. When we love someone, sometimes we put their needs before our own. But love is also wise. It's good to be self-protecting, even when we're with someone we love. Our opinions still matter. Our convictions still matter. No one who loves us should make us do something we do not want to do. That is not love.

14. Someone's First Choice: *Christie's Story*

"Truth and courage aren't always comfortable, but they're never weakness." Brene Brown

Christie struggled with the challenges of going through puberty early. She got her period and developed an hourglass figure years before all of her friends. She suddenly had lots of attention from boys and even men. At first it was awkward, but eventually, it began to fill a need. Christie's father was physically present but emotionally absent, and she longed to be loved.

She'd grown up a competitive swimmer and was nationally ranked by age eleven. Her mom drove her everywhere for events and prestigious competitions. Her mother became obsessed with Christie's swimming career. Her daughter's success became central to her identity, and she began neglecting her husband. She was so wrapped up in the swimming world, she started sleeping with Christie's coach.

Sexual sin destroys us. Makes us irrational. Becomes a compulsion. Christie's mom was never the same. She grew more and more unstable. She abandoned her husband and controlled her daughter. Meanwhile, her husband blamed Christie for him being neglected and betrayed by his wife. Christie's athletic career cost him his marriage. He never treated his daughter the same. She was no longer a treasure to be cherished. She was the catalyst for catastrophe in his life. She was emotionally discarded by the man whose love she needed most.

With a controlling, unstable mom and a resentful, distant dad, the unexpected attention to her newfound figure became welcome. It made her think maybe she was lovable after all. She wasn't longing for sex or even sexual attention, she just wanted to be someone's most important priority. Someone's first choice.

By the time she was in high school, she started dating her first real boyfriend. He was kind and generous and faithful. He made her feel like a princess. Everything she longed to feel at home for years was finally a reality. Assuming this relationship would last forever, she gave herself to him sexually without question. She felt valued and safe.

Until she found out he was addicted to pornography. When she first discovered it, she was shocked. The thought of him looking at other naked women made her feel inadequate. How did she compare? Was she not enough? Why would he watch other people having sex when they were? She felt embarrassed and betrayed. She had exposed herself in such private ways, and now she was just one of many women he desired.

Sex creates a strong bond. It also makes us feel vulnerable. It needs commitment and faithfulness to protect it. Christie had all the vulnerability without the faithfulness, and it hurt. She chose to end the relationship with her boyfriend. She wishes she had waited until she was married to have sex.

If I could go back in time, I would wait until marriage too.

Some say sexual experiences before marriage can enhance your sex life later on. Practice gives you perspective and ideas and confidence. I found none of this to be true. Instead, I associated sex with shame, embarrassment, guilt and physical pain.

That's a lot of baggage to bring into your marriage.

I've met so many young men and women who wish they could take back their virginity. Whether it was taken against their will or it was a choice they now regret, they wish they could change it.

If you have had sex before marriage and you regret it, your future marriage is not doomed. You can still have a wonderful, married sex life someday. It is not an easy journey. For some, like Maria, it is a difficult road. Memories do come back and painful experiences can be challenging to overcome.

Time is an incredible healer. The more sexual experiences I have with my husband, the more those experiences become the only sexual experiences that matter. He is the one who makes me feel safe. He is the one who treats me with gentleness, dignity and respect. The more I trust him, the more I am able to be naked and unashamed with him. Sex is enjoyable now, and it's not about anyone but the two of us. In fact, our physical relationship is one of the highlights of our marriage.

Each positive, sexual experience I have in my marriage causes my old memories from the past to fade. In many ways, it's like those other experiences happened to someone else, a different girl who struggled and suffered and made some bad choices. The young, broken Carrie is an old friend I used to know. But she's not really me.

I am someone new. Someone stronger. Someone whole.

Christie is someone new as well.

Her boyfriend sought help and accountability for his pornography addiction. After almost a year apart, they restarted their relationship, and sex wasn't a part of it. They were both committed to purity, and it made their bond stronger. Her boyfriend proposed after several months of rebuilding trust between the two of them. Now they are able to enjoy the intimacy of sex within the protection of marriage.

Christie's dream of being someone's first choice came true, despite her painful past.

15. Hope Lost

"You don't love someone because they're perfect, you love them in spite of the fact that they're not." Jodi Piccoult

I had dreams similar to Christie. When I started dating Alex, I thought I'd found the love I was looking for. He was so faithful and loyal and kind.

And then my dad came back into the picture. That sophomore year of high school, out of the blue, I finally had a father. It was incredible! Better than having a boyfriend and better than getting a dozen roses on Valentine's Day.

I was still thankful for Alex, but now I had everything I longed for. I finally started to trust this man I had longed to be close to my whole life. There were the Peter, Paul and Mary records, American Pie, and a pink prom dress. I had a father, at last! I could hardly believe it was true... until he abandoned us- again.

When my father left for good, I kept hoping he would come back. Parents are permanent, or at least they're supposed to be. When a parent disappears, hope steps in. Hope believes the situation is temporary.

Perhaps you have experienced this. One of your parents walked out, leaving you there bewildered and confused. You watch them go as your heart breaks and your brain scrambles to make sense of it all.

Or maybe it wasn't a parent. Maybe it was another family member, a close friend or someone else you loved. Someone you trusted. Someone who made you feel cherished and valuable. Someone like Christie's boyfriend.

Hope can't help but see them coming back. Hope refuses to give up.

As long as you keep hope alive, you're secure. You are still loved. The pain will end. This feeling of rejection and abandonment is temporary. You need not become accustomed to it.

Love fuels hope. When we're given love, even small, insignificant doses, we can keep hoping. We can keep believing.

When an absent loved one calls or visits, hope springs to life. The reassurance grows. Everything will be restored to normal, eventually. Faithfulness is not required- not from children or even teenagers. When we're young, we are so forgiving, long-suffering, and patient. Kids are way more patient than we give them credit for.

They wait and they wait and they wait. Their imaginations run wild. They can picture incredible futures full of happiness and joy. They are limitless in their ability to dream. This is why it hurts so much when we finally grow up and give up hope.

As a child, I always secretly hoped my dad would come back to our family. I wanted my dad to care. I wanted to be a normal family. If only he could see that I was a good kid and a listener. I made my bed and did my chores and always finished my homework on time. I was always trying to earn my father's love- even though he wasn't around. I felt I needed to prove my worth.

Maybe it wouldn't matter to him that I couldn't dance or do gymnastics. Hopefully he wouldn't mind that my hair was cut short and people thought I looked like a boy in the third grade. Dad's don't care about those things, right? To them, a daughter is a precious treasure.

And I always thought that if my dad did come back, things would be better. I could go to dance lessons and have nicer clothes and maybe a swimming pool. I would have dad hugs and dad piggy back rides and dad arms to hold me when I was scared.

I had hope my life could be different. When dad moved in that sophomore year of high school, my hopes were finally realized. We could finally have the life I always dreamed of! But then, hope died when my dad walked out.

I had finally opened my heart…. started to let myself believe I was special and whole. There wasn't something wrong with me making my father leave. I wasn't that easy to abandon after all. I was worth staying for. Worth buying a prom dress for. Worth having a picture taken with.

When you choose to open up and are ultimately rejected, your heart fills with hate and anger. You believe those old lies you fought back with your childlike hope. Now you've grown up, and you know the lies are true. You are ugly and worthless. You are hopelessly flawed, and no one wants you.

These were the truths I believed when Dad moved out and never came back.

But they weren't truths at all, just hollow lies I clung to. They were suffocating and damaging. They were also false and weighty.

As an adult, I'm so glad my dad was not more involved in my life. He was characterized by selfishness and manipulation. There was a darkness to his life that I am thankful is not part of mine. My mother is positive and patient. She laughs easily and is characterized by contentment and joy. There is no person on earth I would rather be like. I am so glad she was the primary influencer in my life. And I'm thankful she protected me from the negative impact his ongoing presence would have had on me.

As a child, I thought I knew what I needed most. I was wrong.

16: The Best and Worst of Books

"If you think your failure is bigger than God's grace, that's your second mistake." Bob Goff

When my dad moved out, I started reading his book on my nightstand. It was the only piece of him I had left. I thought it would somehow keep us connected. What kind of books did my father even like anyway?

I was shocked when I came across an illicit sex scene while reading, each moment described in explicit detail. I was embarrassed and couldn't believe what I was reading. I slammed the book shut.

Immediately, I felt guilty. And angry at my dad. How could he give me this book? How disgusting! I was his daughter. This was so wrong!

I went to my mom with the book, infuriated something like this had come from my own father. She told me to throw it away. I went back to my room and put it in my trash can.

Dad's book sat in my trash a while. But I kept thinking about it. I became more and more curious. Were there other scenes like that in there? How many were there? What exactly did they talk about? I took the book out of my trash and hid it under my bed.

It sat under my bed for days. I still thought about it, wondering. I wanted to read it more, but I knew I shouldn't. My emotions swung from curiosity in one moment to shame in the next.

I tried to forget about Dad's dirty book....tried to focus on doing my homework...tried to focus on growing my relationship with Alex. To have something so tempting yet toxic within my grasp challenged my self-control in ways I'd never experienced before.

My resolve completely exhausted, I finally gave in and grabbed the book out from under my bed. I didn't start over at the beginning, or even pick up where I left off. I carefully flipped through the pages looking for trigger words, wondering if this whole book was full of sex scenes. I found seven. I read them all. Nothing else, just those seven scenes.

And I was hooked. I'd found my drug, and it immediately became addicting.

Words are powerful to me. Whether they are spoken or read, they hold me transfixed. The scenes my mind makes up from the words I read in books are more vivid than any screen I could watch. I read those sex scenes over and over again until I had them all memorized.

And I was so ashamed. What I read was new and confusing and intriguing. But then I'd picture my grandmother up in heaven seeing what I was doing and I'd be humiliated. I'd vow to stop. This was my dad's dirty habit, along with his drinking and smoking. I wanted nothing to do with it. I'd get angry and wouldn't read his book for days. Even weeks. And then the temptation would overtake me, and I would read those scenes all over again. I felt owned by a power beyond my control.

The summer after my sophomore year I went to visit some relatives out of town. One of their neighbors was an author. Having always wanted to write, I was enamored with her. She was large and lovely. She brought me upstairs to her studio where she wrote in her home. The room was floor to ceiling bookshelves. It was marvelous!

As I looked closer, I realized what genre of writer she was. These were all romance novels. I was embarrassed to immediately wonder how much sex they had in them.

Then she asked if I wanted to have some of her old books. I knew I should say "no," but I also very much wanted to say "yes!" I decided it would have been rude to say no. She filled a brown paper shopping bag to the brim. It was full of her books and others of its kind.

I simultaneously felt guilty and lucky. I couldn't wait to get these books home and see what they held inside. I never read the stories. I skipped to all the sex scenes. I was obsessed. I enjoyed reading about sex more than actually having sex. Clearly, something was wrong with me.

I told no one about the books. I put them up on my top shelf in my bedroom, which was just inches from the ceiling. There were so many books on my shelves, no one even noticed the large section of romance novels up there. Or at least I hoped they didn't.

The fall of my junior year, Charlie moved out of our house and started living with Papa while he went to community college. Nanny had been gone a while now, and my grandfather had become quite lonely. Our family thought my brother moving in would provide good company for Papa. Charlie and my boyfriend Alex were both headed to the same college, and I was excited for them.

My mind about college quickly changed. Once Alex started attending classes, he suggested we see other people. He was meeting college girls now, and he was curious. What was he missing out on? After two years of faithfulness, he was interested in moving on.

I was heartbroken, again.

No one stays.

Alex and I continued to see each other, but our relationship was never the same. I wasn't enough for him. He liked this other girl, Jane. I never met her, but I couldn't stand her.

Meanwhile, back in high school, this kid, Sam, in chemistry class was super distracting. We both sat in our assigned seats at the back of the classroom. He was always cracking jokes and trying to get my attention.

Chemistry was difficult and boring. Sam became a welcome source of amusement in my least favorite class. He always had snacks, and I was always hungry. We passed notes and told stories and once he drew smiley faces on the bottom of my sneakers.

Sam was always telling me about this thing he went to on Friday nights at his church. It was some kind of youth group meeting. He said it was the highlight of his week, and he would never miss it, no matter what. I'd never heard someone so excited to do something at church.

After months of our back-of-the-classroom friendship, Sam invited me to his church youth group. And on a date to the movies. I said, "yes" to both.

By the end of the movie, Sam was holding my hand. It was nice, but I was uncomfortable. Alex and I were technically still seeing each other, but the relationship had all but deteriorated. I dropped my hand from his when

Sam and I walked out of the theater. I knew this show of affection was premature.

A few days later, I called Alex. Not only was he still curious about this Jane girl, he had become more and more critical of me. He'd be annoyed when I'd splash in puddles or spontaneously climb up into trees (both things I enjoyed doing frequently). Alex would roll his eyes when I'd sing along loudly with the radio, asking me when I was going to grow up. He had outgrown my childlike playfulness.

It was time for this relationship to end.

Sam and I started dating a few weeks later. I went to his youth group every Friday night. I didn't especially like the gym time, but I enjoyed the singing and Bible lesson following it.

Each week the youth pastor would ask, "Who has read their Bible seven days this week?" Most people would raise their hands. I felt stupid. I owned a Bible, but I never read it. I honestly didn't know it was a book you actually read. It always seemed more of a shelf-dwelling book for good luck and dust collection.

One night early on the youth pastor was talking about how real and relevant the Bible is to our daily lives. This was a brand new idea to me. He then shared about a book in the Bible that even talked a lot about sex. He actually encouraged us not to read it until we got married because it could be tempting.

I decided to read my Bible every day because of peer pressure. I wanted to raise my hand like everybody else at youth group. And I knew exactly what book I was going to start with. This was perfect! Bible credit and book sex at the same time.

I couldn't remember the name of the book of the Bible he'd mentioned. I started looking through the table of contents. I had only heard the name once. When I saw the name "Psalms," that seemed like the right title.

I started reading and reading. No sex. I kept reading. Still no sex. I read more. I really liked the book of Psalms. It was so real. The author was extremely honest. He was raw expressing his emotions. His love and passion for God seemed genuine. These strong words resonated with me.

I wanted to feel this kind of passion. I wanted to be this in love. I eventually didn't care that I couldn't find one iota of sex in this book of the Bible. I really liked the book of Psalms. It's still my go-to when I know I should spend time reading scripture but I don't really feel like it.

One idea from the book of Psalms intrigued me the most. This God sounded faithful. He sounded loyal and trustworthy, just like the father I longed for. I wanted to know this God more.

I had grown up going to church and hearing, "Jesus died for my sins," it just never meant much to me. I didn't understand it. I hadn't thought of God as someone who could be known personally, the way I wanted to know my father.

I started praying. Really praying. Not just praying that I would get a good grade on a test or that I wouldn't get pregnant, but praying to know God. Asking him who he was and what he was like.

Sometimes it felt a little crazy, like I was just talking to the air. But I chose to believe it was something more. I chose to believe God was real, that he could hear me and he cared about what I was saying. I found it comforting and reassuring.

I had put my faith in a father I didn't know for years and had found him to be much less worthy than I hoped. What I found in scripture was a God who was full of worth. He wasn't hidden, like my dad. He was longing to be known.

I kept reading the Bible more and more. I loved going to youth group. I loved singing worship songs. The summer before my senior year, I went with Sam and his church youth group to Harvey Cedars Youth Camp on the Jersey Shore. We heard Bible teachings every morning and evening. In between were all kinds of athletic competitions where I simply tried to get by on enthusiasm and self-deprecating humor.

One of the last mornings you could sign up for a sunrise walk on the beach. I'm a big fan of sunrises so I excitedly signed up. Sam was not interested. Nor were any of my youth group friends. They thought I was crazy to wake up so early on summer vacation but I didn't care. I wanted to go. It was a decision I made independent of anyone else wanting me to do it, which felt great.

I showed up on the beach at the scheduled time. I saw no one there. I waited and waited. No one showed. I checked my watch. Maybe everyone else overslept? After 30 minutes of waiting, I started to walk. I had the beach all to myself, and the sunrise was spectacular.

Throwing self-consciousness aside, I started to sing as I walked. I sang the worship songs I'd been learning in youth group. I thought about the words as I sang them and let the truths they contained resonate inside of me. At that moment on that beach, I felt completely overwhelmed by God's love.

After years and years of searching, I finally found the father I'd been looking for. A faithful father, who loved me unconditionally. A father who hadn't missed a single event in my life. He 'd been there at every birthday. Attended every chorus concert. Celebrated every accomplishment. He'd been there the whole time, I just never knew.

He also knew about the books under my bed. And on my top shelf. He knew about my addiction. He also knew about my abuse. He knew what had been done to me. He knew all the poor choices I'd made. I didn't need to keep any secrets from him. He already knew. And He loved me anyway. This thought brought me to tears, and I started to cry out loud alone on the beach.

Many people who have dad issues struggle with seeing God as their father. They direct their anger and hurt at God. They have trouble believing he could be faithful when they've never experienced faithfulness from their own father.

I don't know why, but the exact opposite was true for me. I'd always longed for a father's love. I'd sought it out in so many unhealthy places. And now, here it was right in front of me.

That morning on the beach, I chose to run into my father's arms. I have been captivated by his love ever since.

17. The Search for Normal: *Emily's Story* (*In her own words*)

"Shame corrodes the very part of us that believes we can change and do better." Brene Brown

Seven. The number I will never forget. It is a major marker in my life. I never could have expected what would happen to me. I didn't even know what *was* happening. I didn't learn what was happening to me was wrong or what it was in general until my early years of high school.

I remember the first night. My cousin was living with us at the time. He slept in my older brother's room right next to mine. I don't remember the game we were playing. It was something involving a blanket. They both agreed I would go under the blanket and one of them would join me. Then they would touch me and make me touch them. They said it was part of the game.

I remember just lying there and not moving. I didn't know what to do. Thinking about it now I wish I would have said "no" or said that I felt uncomfortable. I wish I had the strength. I thought it was normal, that it was just what you did. That it was okay. After all, he was my brother and the other guy was my cousin.They loved me. What I didn't know is that this wouldn't be the last time or the worst thing they would do.

I remember being confused and then just going about the rest of the night as if nothing ever happened. But I also remember that was the night that I stopped being able to fall asleep and started fake-falling out of my bed and crying just so my mother or father would come and lay down next to me and sing me to sleep. I started playing more by myself and hiding and playing in my closet with the door closed.

As I got older, I was so confused. I didn't understand why the abuse started to feel good. I was scared because I hated it and I liked it and I didn't understand why. I didn't know what to do. Things definitely were changing. I remember just wanting the feeling and trying anything until I got it.

I remember one night I asked my cousin who was a couple months older than me if I could kiss him and make out with him. He said "no," but I tried to anyway. My other cousin was a few years younger than me, and I knew she would do anything, so I started making out with her. We called it "Frenching." We had seen it in the movies so we knew how it worked.

We would often take baths together because we were still young enough, but this wasn't just play time with bath toys anymore. My mind had been completely changed, and we now used this as time to mess around with each other. This was a regular occurrence whenever we saw each other. I never thought what we were doing wasn't okay. It never crossed my mind. I thought it was normal. I thought it was what everyone did.

My older cousin and brother continued to abuse me. I was terrified that someone would come and find us. But at the same time I wanted someone to come. I wanted someone to see, and I wanted someone to stop it. I didn't cry out. I didn't do anything. I would just lay there still and frozen. I didn't say anything, I couldn't.

I numbed the pain. I numbed my feelings. I taught myself not to cry because I didn't want them to do anything worse. Once after it happened, my cousin told me to put my clothes back on before someone caught me being a naughty girl. I believed it. I felt naughty, and I felt dirty.

My cousin wasn't the only one I tried something with as a result of my experience. There was a kid at my grandma's house. He couldn't have been more than 4 years old. I didn't want to nor did I mean to hurt him, but I did. I often think of him and wonder how he is doing. I wonder if he remembers, and I hope that I can apologize because I never wanted that and it never happened again.

I also did stuff to my little brother. I was unaware that it would affect him in the long run just as I was unaware that what was happening to me would affect me so many years later. And then one time he said that it hurt so I stopped. I felt so guilty. I didn't want to hurt him, and I shouldn't have done it. And I don't recall doing it again either.

I was a Christian my whole life. I knew about God and Jesus. I remember hearing a couple times maybe in high school that sex before marriage was wrong. I felt I was damaged anyway so it didn't matter. I struggled with it for a very long time, and I still do. I found my identity in guys and sex.

Around my freshman year of college, God showed me the need for freedom. I finally realized that I couldn't find freedom on my own or just with the help of my friends. I started talking to mentors instead of just a few close friends. People that could really help me, including a counselor.

God is the ultimate counselor, yes, but he puts people in our lives to help us through things. It's hard but totally worth it. The more the words come out of my mouth, the more free I feel.

I started to see where God had been throughout everything when I didn't realize he was there. People have gone through far worse things than I have, yet they have a faith that's stronger than I've ever seen. It is shocking to me, yet sends me running to God because if someone who has a story so much worse than me can be close to God, there's no reason I can't be.

Through my healing I learned that it's not my fault. It never should have happened to me, but it did. God has a purpose for me and can make good come from this. He can make me pure again. He has made me clean. He loves me. He has always loved me. He will never stop loving me.

I started to find my identity in Christ. I just recently started to get rid of the feelings of guilt and shame.

God is calling us to freedom and forgiveness. This was hard for me to write, but it's bringing freedom with every word.

18. The Birth of Courage

"You will not always be strong but you can always be brave." Beau Taplin

My senior year of high school, I longed to read the Bible more and understand my heavenly father better. I wanted to grow in my new faith as much as possible. Maybe I should even consider applying to a Christian college so I could take classes about God?

Sam and I started an after school Bible study with our high school biology teacher. We attended youth group every Friday night and went to church together Sunday evenings. I could not get enough information about who God was and what he was like.

I longed to be loved as a precious child. I'd carried the burden of guilt for so long, I was desperate to be free. I prayed hopeful, expectant prayers.

And I loved being around other people who also believed in God. They were hopeful and encouraging. I felt accepted, valued and loved by them. I invited several friends to join me at youth group and church, and they started growing closer to God too. We all embraced the feeling of freedom that came from forgiveness.

My new-found sense of community made me more courageous. I suddenly wanted to try new things. Go new places. Meet new people. Something came alive in me I had never experienced before. A sense of adventure was born!

I was so tired of being afraid. So sick of being shy. So tortured by what everyone else thought or believed about me. Knowing I was unconditionally accepted by God freed me from caring about what everyone else thought. I no longer needed their approval.

My opinions grew stronger and my beliefs grew deeper. I started speaking out in class and auditioned for a role in the school musical. I attended conferences and retreats. I started reading books by CS Lewis and became a huge fan of Rich Mullins music.

This new sense of confidence was challenged when Dan broke up with me near the end of our senior year. Up to that point, my faith had been so entwined with his. He was a huge part of my journey with God. Would I lose my closeness to Jesus when I lost my closeness to Dan? I didn't want that to happen.

When our relationship ended, I was sad and struggled to let Dan go. Fear wanted to creep back in. Could I really feel loved without a guy by my side? I had been in a dating relationship for the majority of high school. Now this chapter of my life was coming to an end. It was time to begin my adult life. I convinced myself that this was a good opportunity to move forward on my own.

Looking back, I'm so glad I started college single!

My freshmen year was a whirlwind of excitement. I made new friends, took interesting classes, joined a Christian fellowship group, and found a new church. Choosing all of these things on my own gave me a deeper sense of who I was and who I wanted to be.

I went kayaking, took fencing classes, went for walks in the woods all alone. When I made mistakes, I forgave myself and moved on. I learned to laugh at my own imperfections. I focused on others more than myself and it was freeing.

It felt good to make people feel valued and cherished. I had a new purpose in life- making God's love real and tangible to others, the same way my youth group friends had made God's love real to me.

After freshman year, I traveled almost all summer long. My mom and I went on a trip to Vermont. Then I spent a week leading a canoe trip in the Adirondacks. Then I spent another week leading a bike trip to Canada. Then I spent two weeks in Colorado taking Bible classes and hiking the Rocky Mountains. A new addiction was born, free of shame and guilt. I loved traveling and embraced every opportunity to discover.

I continued to meet new people and learn new skills. I believed in my father's love for me, and it continued to give me a sense of security and confidence. But it didn't mean all my old habits were gone.

Fear frequently tried to win me back. I was so conditioned by it. I regularly fought the urge to run from opportunities that intimidated me. I would force myself to do things I was afraid of to train new habits of courage. I still do this today.

Rejection taunted me. When others laughed in a room, I instinctively believed they were laughing at me. I would tense up and become defensive. Clearly I did not belong. It took practice to remind myself that I belong wherever I wanted to belong. If others laughed, just laugh along with them. Even if they are laughing about me, who cares? Making others laugh had become a goal and it still counts when I reach it accidentally!

I still struggled with temptations about sex. Most of the time, I tried not to think about it. I avoided movies with sex scenes and threw away all of those romance novels from my top shelf. But I still had to be careful. I stopped babysitting for the family with the Playboy and Playgirl magazines because I was tempted to look at them. I continued to think this part of me was broken. How could I still be drawn to it when I hated it and it made me feel nothing but terrible afterwards?

While I had discovered a loving, heavenly father who was faithful and would never leave me, part of me still longed to know my dad. I would not obsess over it like I did in middle and high school, but it was still there.

Like my friend Aubree, I would imagine running into my father in the grocery story or finding him in the park. On my flight to Colorado I was convinced he was sitting directly in front of me on the plane. It was a tall, thin man with short, mousy brown hair and a long face but I could only see his profile. I kept hoping he would turn around so I could see if it was him. And when he finally did look my way, the man in front of me was definitely not my father. I was disappointed.

My life was full and my heart was hopeful, but when would I stop missing my dad?

19. The Only Name Better Than Sweet

"The best way to predict the future is to create it." Abraham Lincoln

I started my sophomore year of college excited about good things to come.

I was now an RA and enjoyed spending time with the girls on my floor. We went jogging at midnight in our pajamas every Tuesday. On Thursdays I led Bible studies in my dorm room. Even though I didn't go to a Christian college, I had a few girls on my floor who were curious to know more about Jesus. I had bought myself a guitar over the summer and was teaching myself how to play.

I joined a new children's theater performance group and was finally taking classes in my major. I was canoeing on the weekends with a bunch of friends and planning a few fall camping trips. Life was full and free and fun.

And then I met a guy. A short guy with glasses who loved to talk and made me laugh and wanted to hang out all the time.

One of my other weekly floor events was called "Rap Sessions." Sometimes I would actually rap, and other times we would all just sit around and talk. Usually, we did a little of both. Each week I'd hang a big piece of paper at the end of the hall and girls could suggest topics for the next Rap Session.

About half-way through the semester one of my girls wrote on the big paper, "What's going on with Carrie and Erv?" And then several girls wrote around it, "Oh yes!" and "We need to know!" and "Excellent topic!"

I usually had plenty to say at these sessions and even had fun coming up with clever rhymes to get the evening kicked off right For this one, I was speechless. They, however, had plenty to say. They were convinced something was going on between us. They listed off their amassed evidence that Erv was in love with me.

Relief swept over me when the hour-long Rap Session was finally over. I was anxious to get out of there. No one would let me leave the room without me promising to ask Erv what was going on. They needed to know. Pronto!

I spent the rest of the evening analyzing and overanalyzing my interactions and conversations with Erv over the past several weeks, wondering if something was there. Did I even want there to be something there? I wasn't sure.

He did have the only last name better than Sweet.

While Erv assured me there was nothing between us (much to the disappointment of my dorm residents), he tried to kiss me six months later.

We both brought a sexual past into the picture, which caused us trouble right from the beginning. Our relationship became physical as soon as we decided to start dating at the end of my sophomore year. It scared us both. Neither of us wanted this to be part of our relationship, but it was familiar territory. We both felt close to God and wanted to honor each other by waiting for all things sexual until we were married. We'd go for weeks honoring our mutually agreed upon boundaries and then we'd mess around and feel terribly guilty again.

As this cycle repeated itself over and over, we'd talk about breaking up. We actually did break up twice- for a whole week both times. We were both so tired of letting each other down and causing each other to violate our convictions. How could we say we loved each other and keep disrespecting one another?

We finally decided we needed to eliminate all aspects of our physical relationship. We could hold hands and hug each other good night but that was it. No more kissing or cuddling on the couch. No more naps or back rubs or late night stargazing on a blanket together.

This was the best decision we ever could have made. Our talks grew longer. Our experiences became richer. Our trust grew stronger. We had to become more creative with our time and our interactions. It set a foundation for a marriage that continues to be characterized but fun, unique experiences (and lots of naps, back rubs and late night stargazing-that regularly becomes more physical and no one feels badly about it!)

*for an in-depth account of this fascinating love story, check out *"Marriage Adventures"* by Ervin and Carric (formerly Sweet) Starr

20. The Phone Call

"Kindness is in our power, even when fondness is not." Mark Twain

A few months after our wedding, my mom uttered words I longed my whole life to hear.

"Your dad called," she casually said.

"He did?! What did he want?" I asked, shocked and supremely interested.

"Surprisingly, he wanted me to give Charlie his phone number. He saw your wedding announcement in the newspaper and was offended he wasn't mentioned."

Wow, I thought. It's been seven years of silence. My brother walked me down the aisle and gave me away at my wedding because my father wasn't there to do it. And now my dad's upset with me for not listing him as a parent in my wedding announcement? Incredible!

"He assumes you've written him off for good so he thought maybe he'd try reaching out to your brother."

"What did Charlie say?" I asked my mom.

"He wasn't interested. He didn't want your dad's number," she responded.

"Can I have it?" I asked.

Moments later, I couldn't believe I was staring at a piece of paper with my father's phone number on it.

I kept his number on a bulletin board near the phone in our kitchen for months. I'd been waiting for this for so long. For years, I'd been practicing in my head what I'd say to my dad if I ever saw him. Now I finally had my opportunity.

I was afraid.

It had taken me years to heal. I had finally moved on. I didn't even bear his name anymore. He was no longer a part of me.

But I still wanted to talk to him. I wanted to know him.

I told myself to be courageous.

Sitting at the kitchen table next to the windows, I take a deep breath. Erv stands behind me, his hands on my shoulders, praying. He knows how difficult this is going to be.

My shaking hands punch the numbers into our push button phone, the curly, tan phone cord stretching out from where it attaches to the wall across the room.

The phone rings a few times, and I wind the phone cord around my right index finger, nervously.

My dad finally answers and I recognize his voice.

"Dad? This is Carrie."

It feels so weird to even say the word Dad after all of these years.
"Oh hello Carrie. How are you? Congratulations on your wedding," he says.

"Thanks. I'm doing well. Mom says you called her a few months ago. I've been wanting to talk to you for a long time."

I put politeness aside. I don't want to pretend. He needs to know the truth.

"I've hated you for years. I was so angry when you left. I can't begin to explain how hurt I've been. You've missed my whole life!"

He listens silently as I go on. He says nothing as I speak. He doesn't try to interrupt.

He also makes no attempt to apologize.

And then I get to the part I most want to say. The part I need to say.

"About a year after you left, I became a Christian. I know I've always gone to church, but this is different. My faith is really important to me now. I've been forgiven of everything I've ever done. God continues to forgive me, and I'm incredibly grateful."

Still silence on the other end.

"But I can't accept that forgiveness and not forgive you. I want to forgive you Dad. Even after all the hurt you caused and anger I've felt, I forgive you."

My father finally speaks.

"You mean, we can start over, like day one? I get a clean slate?" he asks with obvious shock in his voice.

"Yes," I answer.

"I would really like that," he says.

"Me too."

I can't believe this conversation is really happening.

"I would like to see you," he says.

We make arrangements for me to go to his house and see where he's lived for the past twenty years. It's just fifteen minutes from my mom's. He and his second wife are now divorced. He lives alone.

I choose to forgive him, but I also choose not to trust him.

A few weeks later, I arrive at his house alone with a six pack of strawberry kiwi Snapple to place in his fridge upon arrival. This is the brilliant suggestion of my big brother. This time I will arrive as the adult. I will choose when to stay and when to go.

When he opens the door, he looks old. His hair is much more grey, and I almost don't recognize him. He immediately hugs me and relieves me of my Snapple.

The visit is awkward but good. It's the first of several.

Over time, I meet my half sister, who is now a mom. I'm an aunt, and my niece is beautiful. My dad wants my sister and me to be friends.

One day my sister and I make lunch together in Dad's little kitchen. I'm on sandwich duty. It occurs to me I have no idea what my father likes to eat. My sister quickly assists me with Dad's sandwich, knowing exactly which condiments he prefers. I struggle not to feel jealous as I realize she grew up with our father, and I did not.

Our daughter Mikayla is born, and my dad sends me yellow roses at the hospital with a card that says, "Love, Dad." I stare at the card and start crying. I am loved by my dad.

We celebrate Christmas all together. Dad takes us shopping to buy gifts. He gives me a copy of his favorite Mannheim Steamroller album, the one with a blue Christmas tree featured on the cover. It's his favorite because it has Carol of the Bells on it, which happens to be my favorite Christmas song. Spending time with my dad starts to feel a little normal.

And so does the disappointment.

He doesn't always visit when he says he will. He's not always home when he asks us to come over. He frequently calls to cancel. He makes promises and breaks them all the time. He's unpredictable and unreliable. He says he loves me, but I don't always feel it.

I now have a father, but he is still the same man I grew up without.

Forgiveness is not a one-time event. I learn to forgive him, and I learn not to trust him. I need to forgive him over and over again. I remind myself the Bible tells me to forgive seventy times seven. I am tempted to start counting the offenses. Surely his number is up by now.

My heavenly father is still the only one I can fully trust. He is faithful. He is truthful. And I'm glad I know him.

And each time my father breaks my heart, God holds it fast.

21. The Enemy at Home: *Jonathan's Story*

"The marks humans leave are too often scars." John Green

Jonathan hoped his father would be different after they moved to the states.

Unfortunately, he was worse.

From the time Jonathan was a small boy, his father had been angry and harsh. As a child Jonathan watched his dad build a business empire through manipulation and control. Their entire extended family was wealthy, powerful, and well connected. And yet his father always craved more.

They had everything they needed until the trail of corruption eventually caught up to them. Their only option for a fresh start was to flee the country.

Jonathan's family moved to North America seeking new opportunities. They left everything behind, all of their possessions, their wealth and their extended family. After years of living comfortably in a close community of aunts, uncles, cousins and grandparents, they found themselves completely alone. Not only were they in a strange new home where everyone spoke a different language, they were starting from scratch with zero support.

With no one else to rely on, both of Jonathan's parents had to work. Their new home was nothing more than a shack that had no toilet. Jonathan and his siblings had to attend special classes to learn English. The level of stress and anxiety in their home was unbearable.

Jonathan's father took it out on everyone in the family. He was abusive to his wife, to his daughters and, most of all, to his only son.

It started with shouting and cursing. Jonathan was regularly criticized and demeaned by his father. He felt less valuable than the family dog. As he grew older, the abuse escalated. It would come without warning and often without cause.

Unfortunately, Jonathan was also abused at school. Unfamiliar with the language and unsure of how to fit in, Jonathan was an easy target for bullies. His small frame and lean stature made it difficult to defend himself, which infuriated Jonathan's father even more. He was humiliated by his son, and he let it be known publicly and privately.

As Jonathan became a teenager, his father's cutting words and constant intimidation became terrifying. His father even threatened to take Jonathan's life, once pointing a gun at his head to prove he was serious.

Jonathan could not wait to be old enough to be free from his father's control. Though he'd spent every day of his life with his father present, he could not have been more emotionally distant. Jonathan never felt loved by his dad. Though he worked hard at the new family business and had excellent grades in school, he never received his father's approval.

When Jonathan left for college, he intended to treat others the way his father had treated him. It was all he knew, and he knew it worked. He would no longer be manipulated and demeaned. Now he would finally be the one with power to control others.

Those who are abused often become abusers. It is difficult to show love when you have not been loved yourself. How can you show tenderness and compassion when you've never experienced it? How do you express grace and forgiveness when it's never been extended to you? When you struggle to trust others, you also struggle to trust yourself.

Once at college, Jonathan's tactics began to change. He tried to display a tough exterior, using sarcasm and criticism to keep people emotionally distant. He was taken off guard by friends who began to show him unconditional love. Regardless of his hurtful words, they chose to see the good in him. Jonathan was hardworking and faithful, and his friends admired that in him.

Jonathan began to feel valued and accepted at college. He did not need to impress, perform or intimidate. As he let go of bullying and manipulation, he began to embrace unconditional love from others around him.

His friends were Christians whose faith allowed them to be patient and kind. Their own relationship with a loving God allowed them to be compassionate with the unlovable parts of their friend. Even when Jonathan shot them down, they would build him up. They saw him as valuable in God's eyes, and therefore, he was precious in their eyes too.

Jonathan had grown up going to church, but what he learned there had always been difficult for him to believe. All this talk of God being a loving father was too far removed from his personal experience. How could a loving God allow him to suffer the way he did?

But now Jonathan was experiencing something different. The acceptance he felt from his Christian friends brought validity to his Christian faith. He sought God in a fresh, new way. He began studying Scripture, attending church and volunteering in the youth group. He began to combat fears of being rejected and chose to trust that he was loved, valued and forgiven by God.

This made him reexamine his relationship with his dad. Though he still had lots of anger and resentment toward his father, he also looked on him with compassion. What incredible pressure he must have been under to provide? How difficult must it have been for him to start over with nothing? How fearful was his father of failure and looking foolish?

This did not excuse his abusive behavior, but it allowed Jonathan to soften his heart and reach out to his dad. He began to relate to him man to man. Jonathan offered to help provide for his younger sisters and encouraged his father to be more kind to his mom.

Watching his father mistreat his mother has always been more difficult than being abused himself. He would prefer to suffer than see his mother at risk. When his father began treating his mother with greater tenderness and respect, it was transformative to Jonathan.

After years of seeking reconciliation, his father finally broke down in front of Jonathan. He admitted his failures and apologized for the years of pain and suffering he had inflicted. He wanted to be made new, just as he had seen happen to his son at college.

Jonathan told his father he forgave him. He had forgiven him in his heart years earlier. But the power of hearing his father admit what he'd done was emotionally overwhelming to Jonathan. They wrapped their arms around each other and cried as they spoke out loud their love for one another.

It was the beginning of a new season for this father and son. And though the relationship is not perfect, Jonathan goes out of his way to visit and spend time with his dad, even asking him for advice as he starts a career and begins a family of his own.

It had been Jonathan's dream to someday build his own empire. He wanted to become a great political leader or the owner of a multi-million dollar company as his dad had once done. Today, Jonathan serves in his local church and strives to build up the youth, many of whom are refugees seeking a fresh start. He shows them kindness, love and respect, the very things he craved as a boy.

Serving others with the same needs he once had continues to bring Jonathan healing.

22. Conference Confessions

"We know you're strong, but accepting help is its own kind of strength." Kiera Cass

When we started having children, I switched from pursuing a career in teaching elementary school to a career in campus ministry. My life had been so impacted during college, I wanted to have that same impact on others. My schedule would also be more flexible so I could be home with our children.

When our oldest daughter was a baby, I started my new job in campus ministry. We lived in a tiny basement apartment, and I needed to raise money for my salary. I had a large stack of pre-addressed envelopes to give to families and individuals who wanted to donate money to the nonprofit I worked for.

The underside of the envelope flap had instructions and contact information. One day I called the 1-800 number to ask a question of the staff at the nonprofit home office. What I got on the other end of the phone was not the home office, but an offer for phone sex. I hung up immediately, embarrassed and completely caught off guard.

It had been years since I was faced with anything like this. I had been diligent to stay away from both words and images that brought up old temptations from my past. I made sure to not have anything in my home that might trip me up.

This call blindsided me. And it woke something up within me I had hoped was gone forever.

I told myself to throw out all of the envelopes. I didn't need to expose myself to that number again. But I didn't. Within weeks, I called it again.

This was ridiculous. I was married with a kid. I had no need for any of this. This was my past. I had moved on. Forgiven myself.

I threw out the envelopes and forgot the number.

Months past and I was pregnant with our second daughter. We moved into a new apartment with more space. For a while we received the old tenant's mail.

One day a large, thick envelope arrived addressed to "Resident." I opened it during our daughter's naptime while my husband was at work. A catalog of sorts with several loose pages spilled out across the dining room table. It was not the kind of catalog we would ever order from. But it grabbed my attention and held it.

Again, I knew I should immediately throw it away. In the outdoor trash can. After ripping it to shreds. Or maybe burning it.

That's exactly what I did. Eventually. But first, I stuck it in a drawer. Hid it away just in case, like that first book from my father.

I hated being owned by this. I was so sick of being tempted in this way. It didn't even make sense. I was married with a healthy sex life. I was employed in ministry! Why did this desire have such a hold on me? I thought of my husband and how embarrassed I'd be if he ever found it. Men are supposed to struggle with this not women!

I took it to the outdoor trash. And forgave myself. Again.

Months later, I was in Atlanta at a conference for campus ministers. There were four of us, all women sharing a hotel room. Earlier in the day they had announced a special workshop for men in ministry who struggled with pornography.

As we were grabbing our jackets to head out to lunch, two of my female co-workers were joking about the "special session" for men. I was angry. And suddenly felt very bold.

"Not just men struggle with pornography. If there was a session for women, I'd go!" I said. And then I rushed into the bathroom, embarrassed, and shut the door.

Did I just say that out loud? I had promised to never tell anyone this secret, ever. There was nothing I was more ashamed of as an adult.

I waited until I heard everyone leave the room. How would I ever face my co-workers again? One of them was my boss. Would I be able to keep my job? Had I just disqualified myself from ministry? I felt so ashamed to have the ugly truth be known.

But at the same time, I also felt free. We were at a conference learning how to teach students about love and forgiveness. Isn't that what I needed? Wasn't a supportive Christian community exactly the place where I should be able to be honest about my most shameful sins?

Later that day, I was sitting at a breakout session for leaders of small group BIble studies. We were nearing the end of the session, milling around sharing ministry ideas, when one of my coworkers came up behind me. She leaned toward me closely and whispered in my ear, "Me too!" and literally ran out of the room.

She had found a moment of courage, just like I had hours earlier. And now neither of us were alone in our struggle.

We met later that night in a quiet corner of the hotel lobby. We shared our stories with one another. I couldn't believe how similar they were. She too had been sexually abused as a child. She didn't know when it started, but it stirred something in her she'd hated ever since. And she'd sworn to never tell a soul, until I blurted out my awkward confession earlier that day.

We decided to hold one another accountable for our actions. If we were tempted to look at something we knew we shouldn't, we would call each other. And we emailed each other regularly to check in and encourage each other.

My boss didn't fire me. In fact, she encouraged me to lead a workshop for our female students at our next leadership institute. It became an annual class my coworker and I taught together. I was amazed when 20 girls showed up the first year. There were less than 100 students at the conference. We encouraged them to find safe people they could be honest with. We shared the power of having accountability with someone you know and trust.

As long as struggle remains a secret, it has power over you. The more your past stays in the dark, the longer you feel alone. Whether you were mistreated by someone else, made mistakes you regret in the past or continue to struggle today, it's time to stop being silent.

The whole world does not need to know your secret. But you do need to find someone to talk to, someone you can be honest with, and they will love and support you. This person may be hard to find. Fear of a bad reaction can deter you from speaking up. Not everyone has a hotel room of friends to blurt out the truth to.

But I believe God will provide you with someone. Someone safe. Someone who is not characterized by talking about other people behind their backs. Even if you have to pay to speak to a professional counselor who is legally obligated to keep your story confidential, there is incredible freedom in speaking the truth out loud.

One truth I am sure of, whatever scars or sin you are deeply ashamed of, you are not alone.

23. Broken Beyond Repair: *Sosanna's Story*

"Have patience with all things but first with yourself." St Francis de Sales

Sosanna feels shattered.

Her parents divorced when she was just a toddler. Her mother remarried, but Sosanna felt unloved by her step-father.

"Am I adopted?" she once asked her mother when she was a small child. Her younger brother was adopted, and she wondered if she was too.

"No Sweetheart, you're not adopted," her mother gently answered.

"Did Daddy even want me?" Sosanna asked, pleading.

"Yes! He thought you were beautiful," her mother reassured her.

"Then why does Daddy never spend time with me? Why doesn't he ever take me to do things with him?" Sosanna asked.

She felt neglected and abandoned by her step-father. It was the first crack that started her sense of brokenness.

At ten, her older brother sexually abused her. She didn't understand what was happening, but she knew it was wrong. As, she tried to defend herself, she got away, but she didn't dare tell anyone afterwards.

Another crack formed in her sense of self, growing her feeling of brokenness.

A few years later, she found pornographic magazines hidden in her stepfather's bathroom. At first she was shocked to discover such filth, but she was also intrigued. It opened a world no child should experience.

Sosanna locked the bathroom door and looked at every page. These were not just photographs of naked people. They depicted men and women engaged in all kinds of sexual activity.The ideas and options flooded her mind and filled her body with aching heat.

She was angry at her father for lighting this fire within her. How could he have something like this in their home? She wanted those magazines gone, yet they fueled her growing addiction. How could she want something she hated so much? She kept going back for more.

The cracks in her identity grew deeper as she was ashamed of what she'd seen and done. She grew a warped understanding of sex and felt broken beyond repair.

Sosanna started dating early and became sexually active at a young age. She found herself pregnant by sixteen and chose to marry the father of her baby. They loved each other, but they both brought brokenness from the past into the relationship.

Their marriage was plagued by alcoholism, adultery and an abundance of anger. Even after having more kids together, they could not seem to make their marriage work. Sosanna began partying with her girlfriends, trying to numb the pain.

She is not sure why, but Sosanna started going to church. She would go out with her friends on Saturday night and then wake up and attend church Sunday morning.

Sosanna met a Christian couple at church, and she could tell they had something special. There was a sense of peace and joy when she spent time with them. One afternoon the wife called Sosanna at home. They talked a while and then the lady invited Sosanna to begin a relationship with Jesus.

Having longed for love and acceptance her whole life, Sosanna willingly said yes. She didn't totally understand what it meant to have a relationship with Jesus, but she sensed He loved her unconditionally. She longed to know God better and understand who He was. She joined a Bible study and began reading the Bible every day.

Not yet grounded in her new faith, Sosanna met another man. He treated her special and made her feel loved. She knew it wasn't right, but she slept with him one night after a party. And she became pregnant. And she was ashamed.

She was not even divorced yet from her first husband.

Sosanna spent the majority of her pregnancy sick and alone. The cracks of brokenness spread throughout her being. She cried out to God, her only source of comfort.

Her church family encouraged her to finalize her divorce and marry the father of her new baby. She tried to make this new relationship work, but she hadn't recovered from the pain of her first marriage. When her second marriage failed she thought, doesn't anyone want me? Aren't I worth fighting for?

By the time she reached her forties she wondered, why have I made such a mess of my life? Sosanna felt God speak one word to her- pornography. She hadn't looked at pornogrpahy since she was a teenager, yet it had impacted her throughout her whole life. Every relationship she had was tainted by it, but she knew of no way to be free of it. She never considered telling others about it. She was too ashamed, especially as a woman of faith.

It seems broken people are often attracted to other broken people. Sosanna met a new man and married him after a brief time of dating. They were both desperate for wholeness. Unfortunately, she split up with this husband three times in the first six years. Her pattern of brokenness continued. She just wanted to the pain to stop.

Unwillingly to give up on yet another marriage, she and her husband managed to stay together. They resisted the temptation to believe they were better off alone, or with someone else. They were both imperfect and chose to love each other anyway.

Years later Sosanna discovered a program called Celebrate Recovery. Many associate this step program with drug and alcohol addiction, but Sosanna found it to be helpful for so much more.

Sosanna began working with a sponsor who lovingly encouraged her to be honest about her past. She challenged Sosanna to tell her the whole story, even the parts she was most ashamed of. Her sponsor led the way by confessing her painful past to Sosanna. This established a sense of openness and trust. Sosanna realized she was not alone in her pain and mistakes.

First Sosanna put her story into writing. Then she read the painful accounts of her brokenness to her sponsor. The shame started to loosen its grip on her. She began to live her life without guilt and regret.

She found freedom.

24. Say Goodbye to the Air

"Vulnerability is the catalyst for courage, compassion, and connection." Brene Brown

Interactions with my father continued to be strained and awkward. We would gather together for Christmas and sometimes Easter at his home just minutes from my mother's house. It felt strange to split our time between both of my parents. I missed being focused on my mom. She felt so much more deserving of our attention.

My very first Christmas reunited with my dad, I was so excited to be with him. He offered to take my husband and I shopping for gifts. Wandering through the tables of neatly stacked sweaters and t-shirts at The Gap, I was living a childhood fantasy of being loved by my dad. We could choose whatever we wanted and he would buy it.

Erv and I limited ourselves to one thing each, not wanting to take advantage of this "new" family member's generosity. For years and years my long ivory sweater was my most prized possession. It was the first Christmas present ever received from my dad.

My father remarried (again) and we liked his new wife. She was generous and sweet and took good care of my dad. Within months it became clear, he was not easy to live with. As I watched the harshness he showed his third wife, I began to feel grateful my mother hadn't spent the past twenty five years married to this man.

Our second Christmas together was different from the first. No longer trying to impress us with feigned generosity, there was no offer to go shopping. As we exchanged presents it was clear his wife had shopped and dad was not involved at all. We were thankful for the presents but missed the time spent together with my dad. His focused attention had meant more than the long ivory sweater.

The following Christmas, we were not invited to his house. Dad was diagnosed with mouth cancer and hospitalized for surgery. The years of smoking had caught up to him. We visited Dad in the hospital but he was unable to speak. We continued to visit at his home during his long recovery. His new wife cared for him well, helping him manage the feeding tube and various medications. We kept our visits short as we now had a squirmy toddler and a second baby on the way.

Dad made a full recovery and I made another visit to his home. Erv was traveling overseas and needed to be picked up from the airport in New York City. Though I grew up just an hour outside the city, I was not yet comfortable driving there. I was excited when my dad offered to take me. We would spend the day together in NYC and we'd pick up Erv in the evening. Our baby girls would spend the day with my mom.

I was sure I had hit the father/daughter jackpot! My father and I both love musicals and reading. I imagined us spending the day meandering through Manhattan, talking about books, going out for a dinner and maybe even attending a Broadway show. This was going to be one amazing day.

I never imagined it would be one of the most uncomfortable interactions I would ever have with my dad.

We got off to a great start. My dad showed me his preferred route into the city- the Palisades Parkway to the George Washington Bridge to Henry Hudson Boulevard. To this day, it's my favorite, most picturesque way to travel from my mom's to Manhattan.

We stopped for gas and ordered sandwiches at a little deli just before crossing the bridge. Once we got on the Henry Hudson, Dad abandoned our plan of seeing a show and spontaneously stopped at the Intrepid- an aircraft carrier turned museum of military history. I honestly cannot imagine anything I'd be less interested in. But dad was giddy with excitement to share this glorious mass of metal with me.

As we shuffled through narrow grey hallway after narrow grey hallway, Dad kept placing his hand on my shoulder. It was an unfamiliar display of affection from my father. We toured the museum for hours until it mercifully closed. We eventually made our way downtown and Dad put his arm through mine. At first it was sweet but soon became uncomfortable. At times I would try to break away and casually look at something in a shop window. He would immediately grab my arm again and pull me close to him. I was not being held by choice.

When we finally arrived at the airport, we took the elevator to the second floor. Dad wrapped his arm around my shoulder, smiling broadly at everyone crowded around us. As we exited the elevator, he quietly told me, "Those guys are all wondering what an old man like me is doing here with a young philly like you. I bet they're all jealous I'm taking you home."

The affection being displayed wasn't based on love and intimacy between a father and his daughter, it was a show to boost his male ego. I was being used.

Thankfully, Erv's plane was about to arrive. I would soon be back in the arms of a man I could trust.

There was no Christmas gathering at all the following year. Dad was going through his third divorce after another incident of adultery. My father sold his home and was moving to Colorado to be near his sister. We invited him to visit us before he left town. Dad had been to our house a few times before, but it had been years since he'd made the two-hour trip from his town to ours. He would frequently say he was coming and then, last minute, he would cancel. This time was no different.

Several weeks after Christmas, he did show up at our door unexpectedly. I'm pretty sure he had been drinking. His cocky, jovial demeanor was akin to the random visit of my childhood.

He had brought be a belated Christmas gift. It was his old stereo, complete with dual cassette decks, a record player and huge speakers. The speakers reeked of cigarette smoke. He was paring down his possessions before finalizing his move out west. He knew I loved music and thought I'd give the stereo a good home.

I didn't know it at the time, but it was my final Christmas present Dad.

Once Dad moved in with his sister Carol in Colorado, we didn't hear from him much. He called occasionally, but the conversations were strained and the calls became less frequent. Part of me was relieved. Now there were fewer awkward interactions and less opportunities for disappointment.

I was pregnant with our third child when we received a call from my Aunt Carol. I had never met my dad's sister, but she was friendly on the phone and I was happy to hear from her. During this particular call, she sounded concerned.

"Your dad doesn't want me to tell you, but he's very sick. He's been sick for months. The cancer is back. It's more serious this time. It's in his stomach, liver and pancreas. He's checked himself out of the hospital, and he's not going to make it." Her words seemed unreal to me. "You should come see him."

I immediately wanted to be with my dad. He was my father. I struggled to like him, but I still loved him. I'd missed him most of my life. I didn't want to miss out on more time with him. Erv and I already had tickets to Colorado for a conference. The timing was perfect. We would be there in just two weeks.

Though my dad didn't call or feel well enough to talk, my aunt kept us updated. He was encouraged that we were coming. He checked himself back into the hospital so he could get strong enough to see us.

We were busy packing our things, finalizing arrangements for our girls to be cared for by my sister and brother-in-law. We celebrated Brianna's third birthday with a Winnie the Pooh party at our apartment. I decided to pack a few maternity items since my regular clothes were becoming too tight. Erv was at work while the girls and I were at home in our little apartment when the phone rang...

It was my Aunt Carol.

"I'm sorry, Carrie. The cancer moved more quickly than we expected. Your dad is gone."

Just like that.

I thanked my aunt for calling and hung up the phone, my hand lingering on the receiver.

"Goodbye, Dad," I whispered into the air.

I had missed him by twenty four hours. The next day we would be in Colorado, and my dad would gone.

I slid into our tiny apartment bathroom and quietly closed the door. I sat down on the toilet, put my head in my hands and cried. I sobbed and sobbed. The dream of having a loving father was finally gone for good.

It hurt so much more than I ever imagined. The loss overwhelmed me. How could I feel so much pain for a person who had only caused me pain the majority of my life?

Several minutes later, I heard a faint knock at the bathroom door, followed by a little girl's voice.

"Mommy, are you okay?" four year old Mikayla softly asked. I opened the door and let her in, not wanting her to worry. She looked at my tear streaked face with concern, "Why are you crying?"

"I'm just sad," I told my sweet girl. "We won't get to see Pa Sweet again."

She looked at me for a while, and then lit up with an idea. "I'll be right back!" she said, and then she ran out of the bathroom. She was back quickly, her face bright and smiling.

"Here," she said. "You can have my party hat and blower." She handed me her Winnie the Pooh hat and noisemaker from Bria's party the day before.

I put the hat on my head and smiled. And cried some more as I hugged my precious preschooler. Her love was so genuine and generous. I went from feeling empty with loss to full of love for this adorable little girl.

We woke Brianna up from her nap and sat together, the three of us on the couch. WIth one sitting on each leg, I held them both close. I was so thankful for my new little family. For my beautiful girls, for my faithful husband, and a third, healthy child on the way.

I had so much to be grateful for. The loss would not consume me.

There was no funeral for my father. He didn't want one. He was cremated and the ashes were given to my half-sister. The lack of closure made his death even more difficult.

Erv and I still went to Colorado and enjoyed our conference. I visited with my roommate from college who lived in the area but never visited my aunt or my father's family. It was a three hour drive away, and I just decided not to go. I probably should have, but I didn't. I couldn't find the strength to face the emptiness and disappointment I would find there.

Shortly after my father's passing, we learned our third child was a boy. We gave him the middle name Charles, after my brother. My father never knew he had a grandson who would carry on his name.

Our son, now a teenager, has the same tall, thin frame and dark hair of his grandfather. He has the easy-going, patient temperament of his Uncle Charlie. And he has the faithfulness of his father, who never misses a birthday, ball game or chorus concert. My son's father proves to me every day, not all dads are jerks.

25. Everyday Requirements

"Recovery is a street-fight, and our darker side will never fight fair." XXX Church

I'd love to say life has been perfect since I started telling the truth about my past. I've never struggled. I've never stumbled. The wounds have healed, and I'm completely free from temptation and pain.

Unfortunately, this is not the case.

I hate Fathers' Day. It's my least favorite day of the year.

Any movie containing the plotline of an absent father is likely to upset me. A few years ago my husband and I watched "Courageous" at the theater. We knew it was a film about fatherhood, but I wasn't prepared for what would happen in my heart. When a young father decides to start writing letters to the daughter he walked out on as an infant, I lost it. I started crying hysterically and could not stop. I wish my dad had reached out to me sooner. I still longed for a faithful father over a decade after his death.

Kelly Clarkson's song "Piece by Piece" makes me cry so hard I need to pull my car off the road when it comes on the radio or I will be in an accident. It has become my anthem and reminds me I am not alone on this journey of healing from abandonment.

My absent father is not the only demon I face in the darkness. Flashbacks of bedtime abuse still assault me, unexpectedly.

I would not let anyone but the closest of family members babysit my children. When we moved to Rochester, NY away from family, I struggled to allow anyone to watch my kids. Only students I had known for years and trusted like family were permitted to babysit in our home.

We never wanted our children to suffer in the ways I had.

While abandonment and abuse are difficult to overcome, addiction had been the hardest of them all.

Now in the digital age of personal computers and mobile phones, pornography is way too easy to access. I have to be all the more careful of what I see. Social media is especially tricky. Most of the time I know what places and people to avoid, but sometimes sexual temptation seems to seek me. I have a policy to immediately block anyone related to anything sexual.

There are many books I start and never finish because they venture places completely unhealthy for me to go. I've walked out of movies and find way too many TV shows hard to handle.

I have many students and friends share their struggles of abandonment, abuse and addiction with me. It's provided an entire web of accountability, and I'm grateful for it. The more people you trust with your secrets, the more people you have in your life to call you out and make sure you're okay.

There's a reason most people keep their shameful experiences a secret. There are people who will judge us, criticize us and use our past against us. Some of those closest to us cannot handle hearing the truth. It's risky to share the most vulnerable parts of yourself.

Writing out your secrets is a great place to start. If you don't like writing, speak it out loud to yourself. Record it if you want to. Then find a safe person and share it with them. Seek out a teacher, pastor or counselor you can trust. Don't be afraid to tell family. Give them a chance to share your burden. It's too heavy for you to carry alone. Maybe they have been in your shoes too. You'll never know until someone has the courage to share.

Stop convincing yourself it's no big deal. Don't pretend it didn't happen or it doesn't matter. It matters. You matter. Your pain is real and your desire for help needs to be met.

Telling the truth, to yourself and then others, is the first step to freedom. The second step is forgiveness. This is a process. I am still working on forgiving to this day. Someone does not have to ask for forgiveness for you to grant it. Forgiveness does not excuse the action. It does not make what happened okay. It just empties the event of its power over you. It begins to erase the shame.

The person I struggle to forgive the most is myself. I am brutally hard on me. I am the worst bully I have ever met.

I am learning to change the dialogue in my head. I am learning to treat myself with the same kindness I extend to others. I am striving to be my own best teammate.

Don't wait to start your journey of healing.

Tell someone the truth.

Today.

Made in the USA
Lexington, KY
22 March 2018